THE FOUNDING FATHERS AND THE DEBATE OVER
RELIGION IN REVOLUTIONARY AMERICA

THE FOUNDING FATHERS AND THE DEBATE OVER RELIGION IN REVOLUTIONARY AMERICA

A History in Documents

Edited by Matthew L. Harris

AND

Thomas S. Kidd

OXFORD
UNIVERSITY PRESS

OXFORD
UNIVERSITY PRESS

Oxford University Press, Inc., publishes works that further
Oxford University's objective of excellence
in research, scholarship, and education.

Oxford   New York
Auckland   Cape Town   Dar es Salaam   Hong Kong   Karachi
Kuala Lumpur   Madrid   Melbourne   Mexico City   Nairobi
New Delhi   Shanghai   Taipei   Toronto

With offices in
Argentina   Austria   Brazil   Chile   Czech Republic   France   Greece
Guatemala   Hungary   Italy   Japan   Poland   Portugal   Singapore
South Korea   Switzerland   Thailand   Turkey   Ukraine   Vietnam

Copyright © 2012 by Oxford University Press, Inc.

Published by Oxford University Press, Inc.
198 Madison Avenue, New York, New York 10016

www.oup.com

Oxford is a registered trademark of Oxford University Press

Library of Congress Cataloging-in-Publication Data
The founding fathers and the debate over religion in revolutionary America :
a history in documents / Matthew L. Harris and Thomas S. Kidd.
p.   cm.
Includes bibliographical references.
ISBN 978-0-19-532650-5 (pbk. : alk. paper)—ISBN 978-0-19-532649-9 (hardcover : alk. paper)
1. Christianity and politics—United States—History—18th century—Sources.
2. United States—Church history—18th century—Sources.
3. Christianity and politics—United States—History—19th century—Sources.
4. United States—Church history—19th century—Sources.
5. Founding Fathers of the United States—Religious life—History—Sources.
I. Harris, Matthew L. II. Kidd, Thomas S. III. Title.
BR520.F69   2011
261.70973′09033—dc22   2011007137

Printed in the United States of America
on acid-free paper

CONTENTS

ACKNOWLEDGMENTS

We thank the history departments at Colorado State University-Pueblo and Baylor University for providing a stimulating environment in which to work. We also thank the Baylor history department, Baylor's Institute for Studies of Religion, and the Dean of Humanities and Social Sciences at CSU-Pueblo for providing student research support. The editors and staff at Oxford University Press have been terrific to work with, specifically Theo Calderara, Charlotte Steinhardt, Maria Pucci, and Stacey Hamilton. Finally, we acknowledge our dissertation advisers—James Roger Sharp and George Marsden—whose wisdom and generosity continue to guide our work.

THE FOUNDING FATHERS AND THE DEBATE OVER
RELIGION IN REVOLUTIONARY AMERICA

The Founding Fathers
and Religion

It might seem like Thomas Jefferson was destined to become president. When he ran in 1800, he had all the qualifications: author of the Declaration of Independence, a prominent diplomat, and vice president of the United States. But his opponents argued that he was not qualified because he was a heretic. Jefferson had only hinted at his unorthodox religious views, but he had said enough to make it clear that he did not think that one's personal theology should matter in politics. His opponents disagreed. Congregationalists in New England, affiliated with President John Adams's Federalist party, whispered that Jefferson was no Christian, and that his election would mean that America had turned its back on God. By mid-1800, the whispers had turned to angry polemics. Week after week, Federalist newspapers printed an ad urging Americans to ask themselves, "Shall I continue in allegiance to GOD—AND A RELIGIOUS PRESIDENT; or impiously declare for JEFFERSON—AND NO GOD!!!"[1]

Up to this point, the religious story of the election of 1800 might seem familiar, a prelude to today's stereotypical feuds between religious conservatives and secular liberals. But then the

1. *Gazette of the United States*, September 13, 1800.

story took a strange turn: Jefferson won the presidency, thanks in large part to support from America's most fervent evangelical Christians, the Baptists. Freshly energized by the Great Awakening of the 1740s, Baptists had begun to push for the disestablishment of America's state churches. These churches, either Congregationalist or Anglican (Episcopalian), had persecuted the Baptists because they refused to pay taxes to support the state churches, or to abide by state restrictions on their fervent revival meetings. In the cause of disestablishment, the Baptists found a champion in Jefferson.

Jefferson and his ally James Madison, in cooperation with the Baptists, had passed the Bill for Establishing Religious Freedom in Virginia in 1786. This victory set the stage for the adoption of the First Amendment to the Constitution, which guaranteed the "free exercise of religion" and forbade the establishment of a national church. Baptists were among Jefferson's staunchest political supporters, despite their differences with his personal theology. The Danbury Baptist Association of Connecticut rejoiced when Jefferson was elected: "We have reason to believe," they told him, "that America's God has raised you up to fill the chair of State out of that good will which he bears to the Millions which you preside over." They even prayed that Jefferson would find redemption through Jesus Christ, and enter heaven when he died. To these Christians, the election of Jefferson was no victory for godlessness, it was a blessing from God (see document 5:4).

Over the past several decades, the role of religion in the Founding has been hotly debated, as Americans have taken their present-day differences over religion and projected them onto the Founders. Advocates on both sides see the debate as simple: America was founded either as a pious Christian nation, or a completely secular one, in which some Founders might have been privately spiritual, but their religion had no effect on the Revolution, the Declaration of Independence, or the Constitution.

The Founders' religious views were more complicated than this. In fact, they passionately debated the role of religion in American society. But these debates often played out in complex ways that don't neatly map onto our present political divisions, with strange combinations of enemies and allies, such as evangelicals' support for the skeptical Jefferson. In particular, people in the Founding era debated the legitimacy of state churches, the ways in which government might support the interest of religion, and the desirability of theological tests for officeholders.

Some prominent Founders were Deists, men who were influenced by Enlightenment rationalism, an intellectual movement that began in Europe in the seventeenth century and spread to the American colonies a short time later. Though their numbers were never great, they had, as one historian has noted, "the right numbers in the right places," and they "won a surprising following from the eighteenth-century elite." Among them were Benjamin Franklin and Thomas Jefferson, who embraced Deist principles despite their sympathy for the essence of Protestant Christianity. A number of other Founders were influenced by certain tenets of Deism, even if they did not criticize traditional faith as openly as committed Deists did. Many Founders, then, emphasized freedom of conscience, liberty of thought, and religious equality, and they favored morality over dogma, good deeds over pious words, and reason over revelation as the surest way to understand the world.[2] But

---

2. Jon Butler, "Coercion, Miracle, Reason: Rethinking the American Religious Experience in the Revolutionary Age," in *Religion in a Revolutionary Age*, ed. Ronald Hoffman and Peter J. Albert (Charlottesville, VA, 1994), 20–21.

many traditional, evangelical believers would have shared the Deists' beliefs on matters such as religious liberty.

While religion is often divisive, we should not discount the ways religion unified Americans in the Founding period. Whatever their views on Christian theology, and whatever their opinions on the proper church-state arrangements, hardly anyone during the revolutionary era doubted that religion, and especially moral virtue, was important to the life of the new American republic. The most recognizable Founding Fathers—Franklin, George Washington, Madison, Jefferson, and John Adams—were not overtly traditional Christians, but they lived in a heavily Protestant Christian society and took many Christian rituals and assumptions for granted. Days of prayer and fasting, religion-based proclamations, and references to the Christian tradition permeated their speeches and writings. This ubiquitous presence of religion did not even stop when the supposed infidel Jefferson assumed the presidency. The Founders struggled to find a balance between ensuring religious freedom and honoring the important place of religion in American society.

This book will introduce many of the essential controversies over religion in the Founding period, roughly from the beginning of the American Revolution in 1775 to the deaths of Thomas Jefferson and John Adams in 1826. We have chosen to feature documents related to major political controversies of the Founding, often written by widely recognized "Founders" such as Benjamin Franklin, Alexander Hamilton, and Patrick Henry. Thousands upon thousands of Americans—men and women, whites, African Americans, and Native Americans—helped make the Revolution what it was, but we have focused on high-profile statutes and political debates in the halls of legislatures, as well as the personal beliefs of the best-known Founders. As one scholar has recently noted, the term "Founding Fathers" usually refers to "the politicians, soldiers, jurists, and legislators who held leadership positions during the American Revolution, the Confederation period, and the early Republic."[3] For better or worse, these are the people around whom the debate over religion in this period normally centers, and this book offers a brief representative sample of documents showing their thoughts on religion and government. You will find certain lesser-known Founders here, but we do not pretend to have covered all the possible perspectives from the revolutionary era in this book.

The Founders lived in a world heavily shaped by religion. In the seventeenth century, the New England colonies (Massachusetts, Connecticut, and Rhode Island) and Pennsylvania had been founded with religious purposes in mind, usually as refuges for persecuted religious groups in England. The other colonies typically had been founded for commercial purposes, but except for a handful of Jews, it would have been difficult to find European people in the colonies who did not consider themselves at least nominally Christian. Many of the colonies also supported an "established" state church with tax funds. In New England, it was the Congregationalist church, while in the South, Anglicanism was usually the official state denomination.

By the early 1700s, many pastors in America were worried about widespread religious decline. Even in the Puritan colonies of New England, many of the second- and third-generation colonists seemed to care little for the demanding religion of the original colonists. They were distracted by lucrative commercial opportunities, and the British colonies were increasingly swept up into wars with Native Americans and/or other European powers, especially France and Spain. The increasing sense of desperation among religious leaders led to calls and prayers for a spiritual revival. They got what

3. R. B. Bernstein, *The Founding Fathers Reconsidered* (New York, 2009), 6.

they wanted, starting in the 1730s, with the advent of the First Great Awakening.

The Great Awakening was both an upsurge in religious fervor and an attack on the established religious authorities in the colonies. Key revivalist pastors preached the gospel of the new birth, the idea that people had to experience personal conversion and forgiveness through Jesus Christ in order to enter heaven when they died. An "evangelical" Christian, in the terms set by the Great Awakening, was one who believed in this gospel of personal conversion. Evangelicals believed that the Holy Spirit (the third person of the Christian Trinity) came to live in the soul of the converted, no matter that person's race, gender, education, or social status. The emphasis on conversion and individual spiritual experience upset the traditions of many churches, which had previously been very pastor- and sermon-focused. If the pastors in question did not enthusiastically support the revivals, they could quickly find themselves under attack, facing questions about the state of their own souls.

The revivals quickly split colonial churches into factions. Even among supporters of the revivals, deep divisions erupted over the social consequences of the revivals. The radical revivalists promoted public roles for women, children, African Americans, and Native Americans, and assaulted the established state churches as insufficiently committed to revival. Suddenly, the Great Awakening had become not just the preaching of the new birth, but a popular assault on established power in the colonies. This was the greatest social upheaval in the history of colonial America, and it happened thirty years before the American Revolution.

Understandably, a number of historians have tried to argue that the Great Awakening was at least a prelude to, if not a direct cause of, the Revolution. Some, like Gary Nash, have contended that the Great Awakening's attack on established power served as a "blueprint" for the American Revolution. Others, like Jon Butler, have vehemently denied that the Great Awakening had any effect on the Revolution.[4] Most historians, however, seem to agree that the Great Awakening must have had some indirect effect. It energized the religious culture of the colonies and helped give a spiritual vocabulary to patriots who wished to justify the Revolution in moral and spiritual terms. To most patriots, the Revolution was not simply about taxes and parliamentary power; it was about the sacred cause of liberty. The awakenings also gave patriot leaders a new model of popular persuasion. Many of the most famous orators and writers of the revolutionary movement, including Patrick Henry and Thomas Paine, spoke and wrote in evangelical language and cadences, even if they were not evangelicals themselves.

The most direct political consequence of the Great Awakening was the challenge to America's state churches from evangelical groups such as the Baptists. Their fervent campaign against established churches was taken up by Thomas Jefferson and others driven by Enlightenment ideals of religious freedom, creating a massive campaign for liberty of conscience. That campaign helped to end most of America's state religious establishments by the time of Jefferson's death.

The events immediately precipitating the Revolution were not religious, but were political and financial. Americans had reached the height of their British patriotism in 1763, at the end of the Seven Years' War, or the French and Indian War, as it was known in America. In that war, the American colonists had helped the British defeat the hated Catholic powers France and Spain. The colonists rejoiced

---

4. Gary Nash, *The Unknown American Revolution: The Unruly Birth of Democracy and the Struggle to Create America* (New York, 2005), 12; Jon Butler, "Enthusiasm Described and Decried: The Great Awakening as Interpretative Fiction," *Journal of American History* 69 (1982): 324.

in the great victory over the "papists," whom many associated with the malevolent spirit of Antichrist described in the New Testament.

The British triumph in the Seven Years' War held the seeds of the empire's disintegration in America. The British built up an enormous debt during the war, partly due to the exertions required to defeat the French and Spanish in America. They expected the colonists to help pay off the debt, and so in 1764 the British government inaugurated new taxes on trade goods like sugar. This program expanded in 1765 with the passage of the Stamp Act, which caused an outburst of popular anger against the British government. Harassment of British stamp agents made the law essentially unenforceable, and Parliament repealed the act in 1766, with the ominous caveat that they had the right to tax the colonists "in all cases whatsoever." Colonists insisted that Parliament did not have the right to tax them, since they were not represented there.

The crisis with Britain escalated through 1770 and the "Boston Massacre," during which British soldiers fired into an angry crowd, killing five. After two years of relative quiet, a second phase of hostility was precipitated by the 1773 Tea Act and the Boston "Tea Party," in which colonists destroyed British East India Company tea by tossing chests of it into Boston Harbor. The British responded with the "Intolerable Acts" of 1774, which retaliated against the unruly Bostonians by shutting down Boston Harbor to ship traffic, and by replacing the Massachusetts provincial government with a new one fully under royal authority.

The Intolerable Acts led to a new level of resistance among Americans, culminating in the meeting of the First Continental Congress. Although it was originally intended simply to discuss resistance tactics, the Congress heralded the beginnings of a new American political system separate from Britain's. From the outset, the business of the Congress was colored by religion. As seen in the documents in chapter 1, the Congress featured prayers by its chaplain, Jacob Duché, and it regularly summoned Americans to days of prayer and fasting for God's assistance in the crisis with Britain. They also passed resolutions encouraging virtuous behavior among soldiers and citizens, assuming that a sinful people would invite the judgment of God in the war (see documents 1:1–2, 5). The religious influences on the Congress also appeared in attempts by Jefferson, Adams, and others to create a national seal for the country. All drafts of the seal, as well as the final version, included overt religious themes (see document 1:7).

The Continental Congress began meeting permanently in 1775, after the Revolutionary War began. In 1776, Congress began to take up the difficult question of America's independence and formed a committee, headed by Jefferson, to draft a declaration to justify it (see document 1:4). As Jefferson later explained, the Declaration "was intended to be an expression of the American mind, and to give to that expression the proper tone and spirit called for by the occasion. All its authority rests then on the harmonizing sentiments of the day." Its language was rooted in British liberal thought, classical republicanism, and a general theism.[5] The Declaration struck a Deistic tone with its invocation of "Nature's God," suggesting a distant deity who had established the laws of nature and justice. But the Declaration also pointed toward a more traditional view of God with its reference to the act of creation ("that all men are created equal, that they are endowed by their Creator") as the basis for equal human rights. It also referred to God as the "Supreme Judge of the World," and the Congress concluded by committing themselves to the protection of "divine Providence." These references showed

---

5. Thomas Jefferson to Henry Lee, May 8, 1825, in *Thomas Jefferson: Writings*, ed. Merrill D. Peterson (New York, 1984), 1500–1501.

that Jefferson and the Congress wanted to acknowledge God as the creator of mankind, the author of fundamental law, and the protector of the righteous. They included no doctrinal specifics, but the religious assumptions in the Declaration certainly accorded with the "harmonizing sentiments" of most Americans in 1776. These kinds of theistic premises for political principles were widely articulated by the Founders, such as in Alexander Hamilton's *The Farmer Refuted* (see document 1:3). The Continental Congress also did not hesitate to promote the general interest of religion, as when they endorsed the publication of Robert Aitken's Bible in America, to address a shortage of Bibles occasioned by the war (see document 1:6). In the Northwest Ordinance of 1787, they also encouraged new states to establish systems of education because "religion, morality, and knowledge" were necessary for good government (see document 1:8).

Many of the debates concerning the relationship between religion and government played out in the states. Once Americans declared independence, state governments had to craft state constitutions, most of which touched both on religious freedom and religion-based regulations, especially for officeholders. Several of the states also maintained state funding for churches, as they had in the colonial period. These state constitutions (see document 2:1) reveal the tensions between full religious freedom and the desire for religion to continue playing a prominent role in public life. Whatever religious freedom meant to Americans in the Founding period, few wanted religion to become an entirely private matter.

The rest of the documents in chapter 2 show how contested the balance between religious liberty and the public importance of religion could be. The two most celebrated confrontations over religious establishment and religious liberty took place in Massachusetts and Virginia, two of the great hotbeds of revolutionary zeal. Strikingly, the two states arrived at very different conclusions about the proper relationship between church and state. Until the Revolution, both states had official, established state churches: Massachusetts had funded the Congregationalist church (the denomination of the Puritans), while Virginia had supported the Church of England (known after the Revolution as the Episcopal church). Both churches came under attack as a result of the Great Awakening. To the evangelical dissenters, religious freedom meant that government should not give preference to one denomination over another or interfere with individual theological views. The leading evangelical advocate for disestablishment prior to the Revolution was Massachusetts Baptist pastor Isaac Backus, who cogently argued that the patriots should not expect God to hear their prayers for liberty when they denied religious liberty to their own citizens (see document 2:2).

In Massachusetts, Baptists and other non-Congregationalists tried to end the state establishment of religion, arguing that government support only corrupted the church (see document 2:5). In the end, Massachusetts decided to maintain the Congregationalist establishment, but provided ways for dissenters to claim exemptions from the tax. The establishment's supporters argued that there was no contradiction between public support for religion and religious liberty for all (see documents 2:3–4).

In Virginia, the Episcopal church remained technically established after 1776, although the state stopped its funding indefinitely. In 1784, leading patriot Patrick Henry tried to create a "general assessment" for religion, in which people had to pay taxes to support churches, but the taxpayer could designate his preferred denomination (see document 2:7). This would have recognized the Christian diversity within the state, but required financial support to a specific church (exemptions would have been given to non-Christians). But to the evangelical dissenters and leaders such as Jefferson and Madison, who had been influenced by Enlightenment ideals of religious liberty, the general assessment plan was unacceptable. The government should get out of the business of supporting churches altogether, they argued. Madison made this case most forcefully in his *Memorial and Remonstrance* against Henry's general assessment (see document 2:9). The joint campaign by Madison and the Baptists led to the adoption of Jefferson's Bill for Establishing Religious Freedom in 1786, one of the signal moments for religious freedom in American history (see document 2:10). Although the principles of the Bill for Establishing Religious Freedom were ascendant, some Americans worried that this kind of robust separation of church and state would harm religion, leading the country down a path of vice, selfishness, and immorality. A widespread lack of public virtue, these critics believed, would ruin the country and invite the judgment of God (see document 2:11).

The concern for religious liberty and religious vitality also influenced the framing of the U.S. Constitution. Since the beginning of the Revolution, the nation had operated under the Articles of Confederation, but many leaders concluded that the government under the Articles was too weak. Accordingly, a convention met in Philadelphia in 1787, originally to revise the Articles. But Madison and others planned to use the convention to create a new Constitution.

The framers were immediately confronted with the question of what role religion would play in the new Constitution, as well as at the convention itself. In a famous episode (see document 3:1), Franklin moved that the convention begin its daily proceedings in prayer. As inoffensive as such a motion might have seemed, it could not garner a consensus and was tabled without a vote. Even such a simple proposal raised a host of potential problems: How would the convention choose a chaplain to offer the prayer? Would such an action, relatively late in the convention's business, suggest growing desperation? What role should religion play in American politics, anyway?

On the question of prayer, and on religious questions generally, the convention tended to prefer silence and inaction. That meant that the Constitution did not mention God directly, and that the only direct reference to religion (before the adoption of the First Amendment) was the ban on religious tests for officeholders. Then, and now, the absence of God in the Constitution has been a source of vigorous debate.[6] Did the Founders intend to create a secular republic? Or was it an acknowledgment that religious pluralism made any commentary on God too controversial? Or was it simply an oversight? One dubious story recalls that when asked why the convention did not refer to God in the Constitution, Alexander Hamilton said, "We forgot."[7]

Whatever their reason for omitting God, it caused a lot of controversy. As the convention sent the proposed Constitution out to the states for ratification, many critics worried that the failure to acknowledge God would get the country started on the wrong foot. Others were concerned that the absence of a religious oath for officeholders (a test commonly applied in the states) would open the door for non-Christians to enter the government. Defenders of the ban said that it was not meant to promote paganism, but to stop the government from monitoring people's religious opinions (see documents 3:2, 5). Some critics proposed amendments to the Constitution's preamble to affirm America's dependence on God. Then

6. See, for example, Frank Lambert, *The Founding Fathers and the Place of Religion in America* (Princeton, NJ, 2003); James H. Hutson, *Religion and the Founding of the American Republic* (Washington, DC, 1998); and Isaac Kramnick and R. Laurence Moore, *The Godless Constitution: A Moral Defense of the Secular State*, rev. ed. (New York, 2005).

7. Hamilton quoted in Douglass Adair, *Fame and the Founding Fathers* (New York, 1974), 147n8.

officeholders would have to commit to that religious statement when they swore to uphold and defend the Constitution (see document 3:5). But all this was to no avail, and years later, critics were still lamenting how the Constitution ignored God (see documents 3:6, 9).

Opponents did not succeed in adding specific religious language to the Constitution, but after much debate about the wording (see document 3:7) the First Amendment did include clauses on religious establishment and religious freedom (see document 3:8). The Bill of Rights was ratified in 1791, after intense pressure from the Constitution's opponents, the Antifederalists, for more explicit protection of fundamental rights under the Constitution. The establishment clause prevented Congress from creating an established church or religion, although this provision did not prohibit the states from doing so. The First Amendment also guaranteed the "free exercise of religion," a victory for the combined forces of Enlightenment skeptics like Jefferson and his evangelical allies, especially the Baptists, who wanted to stop any form of government persecution of religious belief or practice.

Although the Constitution said little about religion, religious beliefs still shadowed and shaped the Constitution. Some of the framers, including Franklin, immediately began to suggest that the Constitution had somehow been blessed or given by God to America. Others rejected such notions, preferring to see the Constitution as the culmination of America's traditions of political wisdom and reason (see document 3:3). Talk of the divine, or providential, origins of the Constitution fostered the development of a broader American civil religion, in which the Revolution and Founding period were given a quasi-religious meaning. God had intervened to deliver the patriots from British tyranny, and now He had established the nation with the greatest governing document in human history, or so the thinking went.

Religious ideas undergirded the framing of the Constitution, despite its relative silence on the topic. The Constitution's advocates and opponents both agreed that good government had to account for flawed human nature. Indeed, one of the key debates in the ratifying conventions was whether the new Constitution would adequately restrain the passions of sinful men. Madison argued that the Constitution's system of checks and balances would ingeniously counter ambition with ambition, by playing the branches of government off of one another. Henry, the leading Antifederalist, disagreed, saying that the new government was far too powerful to be trusted. Evil men in office could easily destroy the freedom of the American people, he believed (see document 3:4).

If the framers meant to eliminate religion from American public life, one could certainly not tell it in the early years of the new federal government. The first Congress immediately began employing chaplains (see document 4:1). Although this required payments to the pastors who served as chaplains, Congress did not consider this an "establishment" of religion. But later in life, Madison questioned whether these kinds of concessions put the government in the undesirable position of promoting religion (see document 3:10).

The Founders included a presidential oath in the Constitution, and while it did not contain any religious language, many presidents have chosen to swear on a Bible and add "so help me God" after the oath. Even that is controversial: A lawsuit by atheist activists following President Barack Obama's election in 2008 tried to ban Obama from using the phrase "so help me God" following the oath, but a federal judge refused the request.

George Washington was the first president to place his hand on the Bible during the presidential oath. He set other precedents, too. Among them was his comfort with using religious language in official statements and proclamations. In his first year in office, Washington initiated the presidential practice of calling for national days of prayer and thanksgiving. He made the last Thursday of November 1789 a day of thanksgiving (see document 4:2). Although Thanksgiving was only occasionally observed for decades thereafter, Abraham Lincoln reinstituted the holiday in 1863, and in 1941 Congress made it an official federal holiday. John Adams followed Washington's lead and called for several national days of prayer during his term as president (see document 4:5).

Religion also played a central role in Washington's Farewell Address of 1796 (document 4:3). Washington was particularly concerned with the public effects of religion, which he saw as an indispensible support to virtue and morality. Only a benevolent, religious people could sustain the republic, Washington believed. He was concerned as he left office that he had begun to see vicious political factions emerge that he thought would ruin the republic, unless restrained by the charitable principles of faith.

But the fact that religion was important does not necessarily mean that the United States was a "Christian nation." In the remarkable Treaty of Tripoli of 1797 (see document 4:4), negotiated with the Muslim state of Tripoli in north Africa, the United States officially declared that it was "not, in any sense, founded on the Christian religion." No doubt this language was intended to assure Tripoli and the other Barbary states that religion did not pose an irreconcilable difference between them and America, and that the United States was not bound to hostility toward them simply because they were Muslims. But the treaty—negotiated under Washington and signed by John Adams—remains a notable demonstration that, at least for certain audiences, the new government did not consider America a Christian nation at all.

A great deal did depend on agendas and audience, however. The equally remarkable Treaty with the Kaskaskia Indians of 1803 (see document 4:7) secured millions of acres in southern Illinois for the United States while providing government funds for a Catholic church and a priest for the Kaskaskia (who were Catholics already). Although this was a small investment, it nonetheless amounted to federal funding of religion. The treaty was signed by President Jefferson just one year after he famously wrote that the First Amendment erected a "wall of separation" between church and state.

Jefferson, aware of accusations that he was an unbeliever, struck a friendly tone toward religion in his First Inaugural Address (see document 4:6). He also routinely welcomed pastors to preach at Sabbath services in the chambers of Congress, and occasionally attended these services himself. He was in attendance when the evangelical missionary and antislavery activist Dorothy Ripley preached before Congress in 1806 (see document 4:8). Whatever the "wall of separation" meant to Jefferson, it did not preclude holding religious services in Congress.

Yet the battle for separation of church and state continued in the early years of the republic. As we have already noted, one key church-state controversy centered around the possible election of Jefferson as president in 1800. Jefferson tried to keep most of his personal beliefs private, but he was widely rumored to have unorthodox, or even anti-Christian, convictions. Opponents looked for documented evidence of Jefferson's views and found some material in his *Notes on the State of Virginia* (1781), in which he argued that personal religious beliefs had no significance in the realm of politics. His opponents, such as William Linn, a chaplain to the House of Representatives, argued that Jefferson's approach would undermine the religious foundations of society, leading to moral chaos (see document 5:1).

America also began coming to terms with religious diversity in the early republic. Although the country remained heavily Protestant, political leaders knew that other faiths were growing. Probably no one did more to endorse the freedom of religious minorities than Washington. During his presidency, he made a point of writing letters to groups—including Baptists, Roman Catholics, and Jews—confirming that their religious liberty would be honored in the United States. To Washington, Catholics and Jews could fit easily into the republic because they shared a common biblical tradition with Protestants (in the Hebrew Scriptures), and because their religions inculcated virtue and benevolence, qualities essential to the life of the republic (see document 5:2).

Church-state issues also persisted because several New England states maintained financial support for established churches well into the nineteenth century. Evangelicals, especially Baptists, led by Jefferson's longtime friend and collaborator, Baptist pastor John Leland, continued to campaign against the establishments. Leland's 1791 *The Rights of Conscience Inalienable* (document 5:3) called for all governments—including those of the New England states—to stop policing religious beliefs, or preferencing one denomination over others. Leland's argument was born out of evangelical dissent, but its conclusions sounded a great deal like Jefferson's Enlightenment critique of state religions. Although Leland and Jefferson held very different personal religious beliefs, they both agreed that full religious freedom was an essential component of American liberty.

The friendship between Jefferson and the Baptists was on display in the famous correspondence that produced Jefferson's "wall of separation" metaphor (see document 5:4). As we have seen, the Danbury Baptist Association of Connecticut was delighted with Jefferson's election. In their 1801 letter to the president, they acknowledged that Jefferson could not end Connecticut's establishment, but they hoped that Jefferson's victory might signal a rising tide of religious liberty that would ultimately transform the New England states into bastions of freedom. Jefferson was pleased by the letter, especially as it signaled a pocket of political support in a region that was overwhelmingly opposed to him. He replied gratefully, and essentially affirmed his agreement with the Baptists on church-state affairs. Jefferson knew that the First Amendment did not yet apply to the states, but nevertheless he asserted that the establishment and free exercise clauses built a wall of separation between church and state, at least at the national level. He also cited the national-state distinction as one of the reasons that he refused to call for days of prayer and fasting as president. The states, to Jefferson, had primary jurisdiction over religious affairs (see document 5:5). Jefferson never explained all the ramifications of the "wall of separation" metaphor, but he still registered his support for a basic church-state separation.[8]

Evangelical and Enlightenment pressure for church-state separation took its toll, as did the growing reality of denominational pluralism in New England. By the 1820s, the Congregationalist church was no longer the clear majority church there. Connecticut gave up its religious establishment in 1821, and Jefferson rejoiced at "the resurrection of Connecticut to light and liberty."[9] Massachusetts held out the longest, but finally abandoned its religious establishment in 1833. By this time, the revolutionary legacy of disestablishment had been sealed as one of the great political accomplishments of the era. Founders like Jefferson, Madison, and even Adams, one of the longtime champions of establishment in Massachusetts, saw religious

8. Jefferson's metaphor is still a matter of vigorous debate today. Some scholars argue that the separation of church and state has no historical foundation in the First Amendment. Others contend that church-state separation not only provided the basis for the First Amendment but also that the amendment clearly prohibits the government from even the most basic intrusion into the spiritual lives of its citizens. For a sampling of this voluminous literature, see the forum in the *William and Mary Quarterly*, 3d ser., 56 (October 1999): 775–824; and Philip Hamburger, *Separation of Church and State* (Cambridge, MA, 2002).

9. Jefferson, quoted in Edwin S. Gaustad, *Neither King nor Prelate: Religion and the New Nation, 1776–1826*, rev. ed. (Grand Rapids, MI, 1993), 49.

liberty as indispensible to the American experiment in freedom. Adams believed that his overt friendliness to religion in public life helped to seal his fate as a one-term president (see document 5:6).

The union between Baptist evangelicals and skeptics like Jefferson shows that the Founders' personal religious beliefs did not necessarily dictate their views on church-state issues. The Founding Fathers saw personal theology and public religion as different matters. One might assume that only people who held traditional beliefs would want a public role for religion, but consider the case of Franklin. He identified himself as a Deist, yet he was the one who pushed for prayer at the Constitutional Convention. Many discussions of religion in the Founding era seem to revolve around the personal beliefs of the Founders, and this is certainly a worthy topic. But we should remember that the Founders' personal beliefs only tell us so much about religion in the Founding period.

There is plenty of evidence to show that certain Founders, especially Franklin, Jefferson, and Adams, were influenced by liberal ideas about religion and the Bible that emerged from the European Enlightenment. This liberal strain raised questions about everything from institutional religion, to the authority of the Bible, to the divinity of Christ. Deistic notions of God as the impersonal author of creation and morality were more prevalent among the leading Founders than among the general population, but no one religious view dominated among the Founders, other than a general devotion to some kind of Protestantism. The Founders' personal views on theology ranged from Franklin's rather open Deism and criticism of traditional Christian doctrine (see document 6:3), to Henry's traditional Anglican faith and contempt for Deism (see document 6:5).

Chapter 6 offers a revealing selection of the Founders' own views on religion. Some of these Founders are well known, like Jefferson, while others, such as William Livingston, are almost entirely forgotten today. These men held quite a variety of beliefs, and indeed, by the 1790s, religion in America was becoming ever more polarized. Thomas Paine, the brilliant essayist and author of *Common Sense*, became the most aggressive defender of Deism among the Founders by the 1790s, but other Founders, such as Henry, thought Paine's Deism represented a betrayal of the Revolution (see document 6:4). None of the Founders were atheists—not even Paine—but none of the most famous Founders were "evangelical" Christians of the sort produced by the Great Awakening, either. Even the relatively brief number of selections here should show the pitfalls of broad generalizations about the Founders as "secular" or "Christian."

As you read the documents in this book, you will find that religion played a very important—and very complex—role in the era of the American Founding. Anyone trying to project current political disputes onto the revolutionary past quickly stumbles. Assumptions about the inevitable conflict between the secular and the religious do not seem to hold true for this period, or at least not in the way we expect them to.

Understanding the past often helps us see how we became what we are today, but it can also reveal forgotten possibilities. A close look at the Founding reminds us that religion has always played a central, yet contested, public role in America and helps us appreciate America's vital tradition of religious liberty and the free exercise of religion. But it also illuminates a time in which many secular and devout Americans found common ground on both the separation of church and state and a lively public role for religion.

Chapter 1

Religion and the Continental Congress

1. A DAY OF PRAYER AND FASTING, 1776

The Continental Congress routinely appointed days of prayer and fasting to seek God's blessing on the war effort. They envisioned these days as times for repentance of sins and commitment to virtue. These were underlying factors that the founders saw as essential to victory against Britain. But moral complexities lay within proclamations like this one, with its reference to the "savages of the wilderness" and "our own domestics," or slaves. Patriots feared that the British would use Native Americans and slaves to subdue and "enslave" the Americans themselves.

From Worthington Chauncey Ford, ed., *Journals of the Continental Congress, 1774–1789* (Washington, DC, 1906), 4:208–209.

In times of impending calamity and distress; when the liberties of America are imminently endangered by the secret machinations and open assaults of an insidious and vindictive administration, it becomes the indispensable duty of these hitherto free and happy colonies, with true penitence of heart, and the most reverent devotion, publickly to acknowledge the over ruling providence of God; to confess and deplore our offences against him; and to supplicate his interposition for averting the threatened danger, and prospering our strenuous efforts in the cause of freedom, virtue, and posterity.

The Congress, therefore, considering the warlike preparations of the British Ministry to subvert our invaluable rights and priviledges, and to reduce us by fire and sword, by the savages of the wilderness, and our own domestics, to the most abject and ignominious bondage: Desirous, at the same time, to have people of all ranks and degrees duly impressed with a solemn sense of God's superintending providence, and of their duty, devoutly to rely, in all their lawful enterprizes, on his aid and direction, Do earnestly recommend, that Friday, the Seventeenth day of May next, be observed by the said colonies as a day of humiliation, fasting, and prayer; that we may, with united hearts, confess and bewail our manifold sins and transgressions, and, by a sincere repentance and amendment of life, appease his righteous displeasure, and, through the merits and mediation of Jesus Christ, obtain his pardon and forgiveness; humbly imploring his assistance to frustrate the cruel purposes of our unnatural enemies; and by inclining their hearts to justice and benevolence, prevent the further effusion of kindred blood. But if, continuing deaf to the voice of reason and humanity, and inflexibly bent on desolation and war, they constrain us to repel their hostile invasions by open resistance, that it may please the Lord of Hosts, the God of Armies, to animate our officers and soldiers with invincible fortitude, to guard and protect them in the day of battle, and to crown the continental arms, by sea and land, with victory and success: Earnestly beseeching him to bless our civil rulers, and the representatives of the people, in their several assemblies and conventions; to preserve and strengthen their union, to inspire them with an ardent, disinterested love of their country; to give wisdom and stability to their counsels; and direct them to the most efficacious measures for establishing the rights of America on the most honourable and permanent basis—That he would be graciously pleased to bless all his people in these colonies with health and plenty, and grant that a spirit of incorruptible patriotism, and of pure undefiled religion, may universally prevail; and this continent be speedily restored to the blessings of peace and liberty, and enabled to transmit them inviolate to the latest posterity. And it is recommended to Christians of all denominations, to assemble for public worship, and abstain from servile labour on the said day.

2. REVEREND JACOB DUCHÉ'S INVOCATION AT A DAY OF PRAYER AND FASTING, 1775

Reverend Jacob Duché, the Anglican rector of Christ Church in Philadelphia, was the chaplain of the Continental Congress. He delivered a sermon before the Congress, meeting at his church on a day of prayer and fasting appointed by the Congress for July 20, 1775. Duché's opening prayer reflected the common American understanding that the crisis with Britain reflected God's judgment on the sinful colonists. He also expressed hope that despite the violence of the war, which had begun in April 1775, the colonists could still be reconciled to Britain. This desire for reconciliation vanished in 1776, leading to the Declaration of Independence. Duché remained the chaplain of the Continental Congress until 1777. But when the British occupied Philadelphia in 1777, Duché turned against the patriot cause and pled with George Washington to stop the war for independence. Duché became a Loyalist and an outcast and had to flee to England.

From Jacob Duché, *The American Vine* (Philadelphia, 1775), iii–vi.

PRAYER before SERMON.

O THOU eternal and exhaustless source of light, and life, and love! In thee we live and move and have our being! Every moment deals to us a portion of thy bounty, and demands the tribute of unceasing praise! Thy name is LOVE! And LOVE the essence of thy nature! The religion thou hast taught us is a religion of love! And love is the principle and end of all thy dispensations!

NEVER dost thou send thy judgments abroad into the world, never dost thou suffer thy chastising hand to fall heavy upon thy children, but when they become insensible of that endearing relation, in which they stand to thee and to each other, and thus violate thy eternal living law of love!

WE acknowledge, therefore, and adore thy wisdom and goodness in the infliction of national punishments upon national guilt! Our eyes must be blinded, and our hearts hardened indeed, if we do not see and feel, under our present visitation, the manifest tokens of thy divine displeasure!

WE own and lament, that the dark cloud of judgment, which now hangs over our heads, hath risen from our unnumbered sins and rebellions against thee! Against thee only have we sinned! To thee only have we been disobedient and ungrateful. We have neglected to improve under thy past corrections. We have shamefully slighted thy past loving-kindnesses. Our prosperity hath rendered us forgetful of thee our GOD, regardless of thine holy ordinances, inattentive to the precepts of thy gospel!

BUT yet, spare us, good LORD, spare thy people, whom thou hast redeemed, and let not thine heritage be brought to confusion! Recall thy ministers of vengeance! And put a stop to the unnatural effusion of christian blood!

FROM our present grievous calamities, not our merits, but thy mercy, not our foresight but thy providence alone can deliver us. Accept, therefore, the prayers and supplications, that have this day been offered at the foot-stool of thy throne! Accept, for thy WELL-BELOVED's sake, our public acts of penitence and humiliation!

GIVE us grace seriously to lay to heart the great danger we are in from our present unhappy divisions! Take away all hatred, bitterness and resentment from our breasts. Enable us to forgive our offending BRETHREN, even as we ourselves look for forgiveness at the hands of our offended GOD!

AND O thou, who alone canst make men to be of one mind in an house! Restore that brotherly union and concord, which ought ever to subsist inviolate in the great family to which we belong! And as there is but one body, and one spirit, and one hope of our calling, one LORD, one faith, one baptism, one GOD and FATHER of us all,[1] so may we henceforth be all of one heart and of one soul, united in one holy bond of truth and peace, of faith and charity!

3. ALEXANDER HAMILTON ON GOD-GIVEN RIGHTS, 1775

The Declaration's notion that God gave people inalienable rights was becoming more common among Americans in the revolutionary era, because it gave them a way to appeal to a higher law than that of the British government. Alexander Hamilton, then a student

---

1. Ephesians 4:4–6.

at King's College (later Columbia) in New York City, explained the basis for natural law and human rights in the pamphlet *The Farmer Refuted*. He derived his understanding of natural law from the celebrated English legal scholar William Blackstone, whose *Commentaries on the Laws of England* (1765–1769) Hamilton quotes here.

From Alexander Hamilton, *The Farmer Refuted* (New York, 1775), 6, 38.

... the deity, from the relations, we stand in, to himself and to each other, has constituted an eternal and immutable law, which is, indispensibly, obligatory upon all mankind, prior to any human institution whatever.

This is what is called the law of nature, "which, being coeval with mankind, and dictated by God himself, is, of course, superior in obligation to any other. It is binding over all the globe, in all countries, and at all times. No human laws are of any validity, if contrary to this; and such of them as are valid, derive all their authority, mediately, or immediately, from this original." BLACKSTONE.

Upon this law, depend the natural rights of mankind, the supreme being gave existence to man, together with the means of preserving and beautifying that existence. He endowed him with rational faculties, by the help of which, to discern and pursue such things, as were consistent with his duty and interest, and invested him with an inviolable right to personal liberty, and personal safety.

Hence, in a state of nature, no man had any *moral* power to deprive another of his life, limbs, property or liberty; nor the least authority to command, or exact obedience from him; except that which arose from the ties of consanguinity.[2]

---

2. Relationship by blood.

Hence also, the origin of all civil government, justly established, must be a voluntary compact, between the rulers and the ruled; and must be liable to such limitations, as are necessary for the security of the *absolute rights* of the latter; for what original title can any man or set of men have, to govern others, except their own consent? To usurp dominion over a people, in their own despite, or to grasp at a more extensive power than they are willing to entrust, is to violate that law of nature, which gives every man a right to his personal liberty, and can, therefore, confer no obligation to obedience . . .

The sacred rights of mankind are not to be rummaged for, among old parchments, or musty records. They are written, as with a sun beam, in the whole *volume* of human nature, by the hand of the divinity itself; and can never be erased or obscured by mortal power.

4. DECLARATION OF INDEPENDENCE, 1776

More than a year after the war between Britain and the colonies began, the Continental Congress declared independence. On July 4, 1776, the Congress adopted this Declaration drafted by a committee headed by Thomas Jefferson. Although much of the document focuses on the specific grievances of the Congress against King George III, the Declaration begins and ends with references to the natural law of God, rights given by God, the justice of God, and divine providence. An appeal to God's purposes justified the American Revolution as a cause much greater than disputes over taxes or the jurisdictions of British and colonial legislatures.

From the *New York Journal*, July 11, 1776.

When in the course of human events, it becomes necessary for one people to dissolve the political bands which have connected them with another, and to assume among the powers of the earth, the separate and equal station to which the laws of nature and of nature's God entitle them, a decent respect to the opinions of mankind requires that they should declare the causes which impel them to the separation.

We hold these truths to be self-evident, that all men are created equal, that they are endowed by their Creator with certain unalienable rights, that among these are Life, Liberty and the Pursuit of Happiness . . .

We, therefore, the Representatives of the UNITED STATES OF AMERICA, in General Congress assembled, appealing to the Supreme Judge of the world for the rectitude of our intentions, do, in the name and by the authority of the good people of these Colonies, solemnly publish and declare, That these United Colonies are, and of right ought to be, Free and Independent States; that they are absolved from all allegiance to the British Crown, and that all political connection between them and the State of Great Britain, is and ought to be totally dissolved; and that as Free and Independent States, they have full power to levy war, conclude peace, contract alliances, establish Commerce, and to do all other acts and things which Independent States may of right do. And for the support of this declaration, with a firm reliance on the protection of Divine Providence we mutually pledge to each other our lives, our fortunes, and our sacred honour.

5. A RESOLUTION FOR TRUE RELIGION AND GOOD MORALS, 1778

Many leading patriots were convinced that their fortunes in the war would rise and fall on their commitment to morality. Providence judged nations according to their goodness, they believed. Accordingly, the Congress passed a resolution in 1778 recommending measures to discourage sinfulness, especially in the army.

> From Continental Congress, *Journals of Congress, containing the proceedings from January 1, 1778, to January 1, 1779* (Philadelphia, 1779), 590.
>
> Whereas true religion and good morals are the only solid foundations of public liberty and happiness:
>
> *Resolved,* That it be and it is hereby earnestly recommended to the several states to take the most effectual measures for the encouragement thereof, and for the suppressing theatrical entertainments, horse-racing, gaming, and such other diversions as are productive of idleness, dissipation, and a general depravity of principles and manners.
>
> *Resolved,* That all officers in the army of the United States be and hereby are strictly enjoined to see that the good and wholesome rules provided for the discountenancing of prophaneness and vice, and the preservation of morals among the soldiers, are duly and punctually observed.

6. ROBERT AITKEN'S BIBLE, 1781–1782

Bibles were in short supply during the War for Independence. Americans could no longer import Bibles from Great Britain, their primary supplier. Consequently, a group of ministers petitioned the

Congress in 1777 to address this shortage. A congressional committee comprised of James Duane of New York, Thomas McKean of Delaware, and John Witherspoon of New Jersey recommended that the Congress import twenty thousand Bibles from "Scotland, Holland, or elsewhere" but provided no funds to do so. Alarmed at this development, Robert Aitken, a noted Presbyterian elder and prominent Philadelphia bookseller, asked Congress for permission to publish a Bible in the English language. Congress supported the request, but did not provide funds to assist Aitken.

From Aitken's Petition, January 21, 1781, *Papers of the Continental Congress*, item no. 41, I, folio 63, Library of Congress; Congressional Endorsement of Aitken's Bible, September 12, 1782, Worthington Chauncey Ford, ed., *Journals of the Continental Congress, 1774–1789* (Washington, DC, 1906), 23:572–574.

Aitken's Petition (January 21, 1781)

To the Honourable The Congress of the United States of America
The Memorial of Robert Aitken of the City of Philadelphia, Printer

Humbly Sheweth

That in every well regulated Government in Christendom The Sacred Books of the Old and New Testament, commonly called the Holy Bible, are printed and published under the Authority of the Sovereign Powers, in order to prevent the fatal confusion that would arise, and the alarming Injuries the Christian Faith might suffer from the spurious and erroneous Editions of Divine Revelation. That your Memorialist has no doubt but this work is an Object worthy the attention of the Congress of the United States of America, who will not neglect spiritual security, while they are virtuously contending for temporal blessings. Under this persuasion your Memorialist begs leave to inform your Honours that he both begun and made considerable progress in a neat Edition of the Holy Scriptures for the use of schools, But being cautious of suffering his copy of the Bible to Issue forth without the sanction of Congress, Humbly prays that your Honours would take this important matter into serious consideration & would be pleased to appoint one Member or Members of your Honourable Body to inspect his work so that the same may be published under the Authority of Congress. And further, your Memorialist prays, that he may be Commissioned or otherwise appointed & Authorized to print and vend Editions of, the Sacred Scriptures, in such manner and form as my best suit the wants and demands of the good people of these States, provided the same be in all things perfectly consonant to the Scriptures as heretofore Established and received amongst us.

And as in Duty bound your Memorialist shall ever pray.

Robt³ Aitken

Congressional Endorsement of Aitken's Bible
(September 12, 1782)

The committee, consisting of Mr. [James] Duane, Mr. [Thomas] McKean and Mr. [John] Witherspoon, to whom was referred a memorial of Robert Aitken, printer, dated January 21, 1781, respecting an edition of the holy scriptures, report,

That Mr. Aitken has at a great expence now finished an American edition of the holy scriptures in English; that the committee have, from time to time, attended to his progress in the work: that they also recommended it to the two

---

3. Robert.

chaplains of Congress to examine and give their opinion of the execution, who have accordingly reported thereon:

The recommendation and report being as follows:

PHILADELPHIA, *1 September, 1782*

Rev. Gentlemen, Our knowledge of your piety and public spirit leads us without apology to recommend to your particular attention the edition of the holy scriptures publishing by Mr. Aitken. He undertook this expensive work at a time, when from the circumstances of the war, an English edition of the Bible could not be imported, nor any opinion formed how long the obstruction might continue. On this account particularly he deserves applause and encouragement. We therefore wish you, reverend gentlemen, to examine the execution of the work, and if approved, to give it the sanction of your judgment and the weight of your recommendation. We are with very great respect, your most obedient humble servants,

(Signed) JAMES DUANE, *Chairman,*

In behalf of a committee of Congress on Mr. Aitken's memorial.

Rev. Dr. White and Rev. Mr. Duffield, chaplain of the United States in Congress assembled.

REPORT

Gentlemen, Agreeably to your desire, we have paid attention to Mr. Robert Aitken's impression of the holy scriptures, of the old and new testament. Having selected and examined a variety of passages throughout the work, we are of opinion, that it is executed with great accuracy as to the sense, and with as few grammatical and typographical errors as could be expected in an undertaking of such magnitude. Being ourselves witnesses of the demand for this invaluable book, we rejoice in the present prospect of a supply, hoping that it will prove as advantageous as it is honorable to the gentleman, who has exerted himself to furnish it at the evident risk of private fortune. We are, gentlemen, your very respectful and humble servants,

(Signed) WILLIAM WHITE

GEORGE DUFFIELD

PHILADELPHIA, September 10, 1782.

Hon. James Duane, esq. chairman, and the other hon. gentlemen of the committee of Congress on Mr. Aitken's memorial.

Whereupon, Resolved, That the United States in Congress assembled, highly approve the pious and laudable undertaking of Mr. Aitken, as subservient to the interest of religion as well as an instance of the progress of arts in this country, and being satisfied from the above report, of his care and accuracy in the execution of the work, they recommend this edition of the Bible to the inhabitants of the United States, and hereby authorise him to publish this recommendation in the manner he shall think proper.

7. DESIGNING A NATIONAL SEAL, 1782

Immediately after declaring independence, the Continental Congress commissioned Ben Franklin, Thomas Jefferson, and John Adams to design a national seal that would serve as a symbol and coat of arms for the new nation. From the beginning, suggested features of the seal included religious themes. Franklin and Jefferson both proposed scenes from the Old Testament book of Exodus, in which the people of Israel were led by God out of captivity in Egypt. When the three Founders could not settle on a design, they contracted a Philadelphia artist who designed a seal that included a radiant "eye of Providence" at its top. But the Congress did not approve

Figure 1.1 Image of seal from *The Columbian Magazine* (1786) http://commons.wikimedia.org/wiki/File:Trenchard_1786_Great_Seal_Reverse.jpg

the proposed seal. A second committee in 1780 also failed to produce an acceptable design.

Finally, in 1782, the Congress's secretary, Charles Thomson, modified the recommendations of a third committee in order to produce a seal that Congress approved. The reverse side of the seal maintained clear religious themes, with the eye of Providence hovering over an unfinished pyramid. It also featured the Latin mottoes "Annuit Coeptis" (God has favored our undertakings) and "Novus Ordo Seclorum" (a new order of the ages). The former motto affirmed Americans' sense that God had repeatedly intervened on America's behalf through Providence. Thomson wrote that the "pyramid signifies strength and duration: the eye over it and the motto allude to the many signal interpositions of providence in favor of the American cause." The Great Seal has a number of ceremonial and diplomatic uses, and since 1935 it has appeared on the back of one-dollar bills.

8. THE NORTHWEST ORDINANCE, 1787

The Northwest Ordinance, one of the signature accomplishments of the Confederation Congress, created the first organized territory in the United States. As land speculators moved into the lands between the Ohio and Mississippi rivers, the Congress outlined parameters for the formation of new states in this region. Most notably, as this excerpt shows, Congress was concerned about religion in the territory, claiming that "Religion, Morality, and knowledge [were] necessary to good government and the happiness of mankind." Therefore, they recommended that each new state within the territory provide for a system of education.

From Worthington Chauncey Ford, ed., *Journals of the Continental Congress, 1774–1789* (Washington, DC, 1906), 32: 334, 339–341.

An Ordinance for the Government of the Territory of the United States, North-West of the River Ohio [Northwest Ordinance] (July 1787)

And for extending the fundamental principles of civil and religious liberty, which form the basis whereon these republics, their laws and constitutions are erected; to fix and establish those principles as the basis of all laws, constitutions and governments, which forever hereafter shall be formed in the said territory; to provide also for the establishment of States and permanent government therein, and for their admission to a share in the federal Councils[4] on an equal footing with the original States, at as early periods as may be consistent with the general interest,

It is hereby Ordained and declared by the authority aforesaid, That the following Articles shall be considered as Articles of compact between the Original States and the people and States in the said territory, and forever remain unalterable, unless by common consent, *to wit*,

Article the First. No person demeaning himself in a peaceable and orderly manner shall ever be molested on account of his mode of worship or religious sentiments in the said territory.…

Article the Third. Religion, Morality *and knowledge being necessary to good government and the happiness of mankind*, Schools and the means of education shall forever be encouraged. The utmost good faith shall always be observed towards the Indians, their lands and property shall never be taken from them without their consent; and in their property, rights and liberty, they never shall be invaded or disturbed, unless in just and lawful wars authorised by Congress; but laws founded in justice and humanity shall from time to time be made, for preventing wrongs being done to them, and for preserving peace and friendship with them.

4. Government.

Chapter 2

Religion and State Governments

1. STATE CONSTITUTIONS, 1776–1778

Once Americans declared independence in 1776, the colonies became states and set about drafting new constitutions. The state constitutions explored new legal arrangements for religion and church-state relations. This sample of state constitutions, adopted between 1776 and 1778, typically included declarations of rights, including statements on the unalienable right of conscience, or the right to worship God according to one's own convictions. But they also often included religious oaths for officeholders, and various forms of religious establishments, or state support for religion. Some also allowed exemptions of conscience for dissenting religious groups like the Quakers, who opposed military service and oath-taking. The religious provisions of the state constitutions reflected Americans' desire to balance the public importance of religion with the need for freedom of conscience.

From Francis Newton Thorpe, ed., *The Federal and State Constitutions, Colonial Charters, and Other Organic Laws of the States,*

Territories, and Colonies Now or Heretofore Forming the United States of America, 7 vols. (Washington, DC, 1909), 5:3082–3085; 5:2636–2637; 6:3255–3257; 5:2788, 2793; 6:3740, 3742–3743; 3:1689–1690.

Pennsylvania Constitution, *September 28, 1776*

Declaration of Rights

II. That all men have a natural and unalienable right to worship Almighty God according to the dictates of their own consciences and understanding: And that no man ought or of right can be compelled to attend any religious worship, or erect or support any place of worship, or maintain any ministry, contrary to, or against, his own free will and consent: Nor can any man, who acknowledges the being of a God, be justly deprived or abridged of any civil right as a citizen, on account of his religious sentiments or peculiar mode of religious worship: And that no authority can or ought to be vested in, or assumed by any power whatever, that shall in any case interfere with, or in any manner controul, the right of conscience in the free exercise of religious worship.

PLAN OR FRAME OF GOVERNMENT FOR THE COMMONWEALTH OR STATE OF PENNSYLVANIA

SECT. 10.

. . . each member,[1] before he takes his seat, shall make and subscribe the following declaration, viz:

I do believe in one God, the creator and governor of the universe, the rewarder of the good and the punisher of the wicked. And I do acknowledge the Scriptures of the Old and New Testament to be given by Divine inspiration.

1. Of the House of Representatives of Pennsylvania.

And no further or other religious test shall ever hereafter be required of any civil officer or magistrate in this State.

New York Constitution, *April 20, 1777*

XXXVIII. And whereas we are required, by the benevolent principles of rational liberty, not only to expel civil tyranny, but also to guard against that spiritual oppression and intolerance wherewith the bigotry and ambition of weak and wicked priests and princes have scourged mankind, this convention doth further, in the name and by the authority of the good people of this State, ordain, determine, and declare, that the free exercise and enjoyment of religious profession and worship, without discrimination or preference, shall forever hereafter be allowed, within this State, to all mankind: *Provided,* That the liberty of conscience, hereby granted, shall not be so construed as to excuse acts of licentiousness, or justify practices inconsistent with the peace or safety of this State.

XXXIX. And whereas the ministers of the gospel are, by their profession, dedicated to the service of God and the care of souls, and ought not to be diverted from the great duties of their function; therefore, no minister of the gospel, or priest of any denomination whatsoever, shall, at any time hereafter, under any presence or description whatever, be eligible to, or capable of holding, any civil or military office or place within this State.

XL. And whereas it is of the utmost importance to the safety of every State that it should always be in a condition of defence; and it is the duty of every man who enjoys the protection of society to be prepared and willing to defend it; this convention therefore, in the name and by the authority of the good people of this State, doth ordain, determine, and declare that the militia of this State, at all times hereafter, as well in peace as in war, shall be armed and disciplined, and in readiness for service. That all such of the inhabitants of this State being of the people called Quakers as, from scruples of conscience, may be averse to the bearing of arms, be therefrom excused by the legislature; and do pay to the State such sums of money, in lieu of their personal service, as the same may, in the judgment of the legislature, be worth.

South Carolina Constitution, March 19, 1778

XXXVIII. That all persons and religious societies who acknowledge that there is one God, and a future state of rewards and punishments, and that God is publicly to be worshipped, shall be freely tolerated. The Christian Protestant religion shall be deemed, and is hereby constituted and declared to be, the established religion of this State. That all denominations of Christian Protestants in this State, demeaning themselves peaceably and faithfully, shall enjoy equal religious and civil privileges. To accomplish this desirable purpose without injury to the religious property of those societies of Christians which are by law already incorporated for the purpose of religious worship, and to put it fully into the power of every other society of Christian Protestants, either already formed or hereafter to be formed, to obtain the like incorporation, it is hereby constituted, appointed, and declared that the respective societies of the Church of England that are already formed in this State for the purpose of religious worship shall still continue incorporate and hold the religious property now in their possession. And that whenever fifteen or more male persons, not under twenty-one years of age, professing the Christian Protestant religion, and agreeing to unite themselves in a society for the purposes of religious worship, they shall, (on complying with the terms hereinafter mentioned,) be, and be constituted a church, and be esteemed and regarded in law as of the established religion of the State, and on a petition to the legislature shall be entitled to be incorporated and to enjoy equal privileges. That every society of Christians so formed shall give themselves a name or denomination by which they shall be called and known in law, and all that associate with them for the purposes of worship shall be esteemed as belonging to the society so called. But that previous to the establishment and incorporation of the respective societies of every denomination as aforesaid, and in order to entitle them thereto, each society so petitioning shall have agreed to and subscribed in a book the following five articles, without which no agreement or union of men upon pretence of religion shall entitle them to be incorporated and esteemed as a church of the established religion of this State:

1st. That there is one eternal God, and a future state of rewards and punishments.

2d. That God is publicly to be worshipped.

3d. That the Christian religion is the true religion.

4th. That the holy scriptures of the Old and New Testaments are of divine inspiration, and are the rule of faith and practice.

5th. That it is lawful and the duty of every man being thereunto called by those that govern, to bear witness to the truth.

And that every inhabitant of this State, when called to make an appeal to God as a witness to truth, shall be permitted to do it in that way which is most agreeable to the dictates of his own conscience. And that the people of this State may forever enjoy the right of electing their own pastors or clergy, and at the same time that the State may have sufficient security for the due discharge of the pastoral office, by those who shall be admitted to be clergymen, no person shall officiate as minister of any established church who shall not have been chosen by a majority of the society to which he shall minister, or by persons appointed by the said majority, to choose and procure a minister for them; nor until the minister so chosen and appointed shall have made and subscribed to the following declaration, over and above the aforesaid five articles, viz: "That he is determined by God's grace out of the holy scriptures, to instruct the people committed to his charge, and to teach nothing as required of necessity to eternal salvation but that which he shall be persuaded may be concluded and proved from the scripture; that he will use both public and private admonitions, as well to the sick as to the whole within his cure, as need shall require and occasion shall be given, and that he will be diligent in prayers, and in reading of the same; that he will be diligent to frame and fashion his own self and his family according to the doctrine of Christ, and to make both himself and them, as much as in him lieth, wholesome examples and patterns to the flock of Christ; that he will maintain and set forwards, as much as he can, quietness, peace, and love among all people, and especially among those that are or shall be committed to his charge.["] No person shall disturb or molest any religious assembly; nor shall use any reproachful, reviling, or abusive language against any church, that being the certain way of disturbing the peace, and of hindering the conversion of any to the truth, by engaging them in quarrels and animosities, to the hatred of the professors, and that profession which otherwise they might be brought to assent to. No person whatsoever shall speak anything in their religious assembly irreverently or seditiously of the government of this State. No person shall, by law, be obliged to pay towards the maintenance and support of a religious worship that he does not freely join in, or has not voluntarily engaged to support. But the churches, chapels, parsonages, glebes,[2] and all other property now belonging to any societies of the Church of England, or any other religious societies, shall remain and be secured to them forever. The poor shall be supported, and elections managed in the accustomed manner, until laws shall be provided to adjust those matters in the most equitable way.

North Carolina Constitution, *December 18, 1776*

Declaration of Rights

XIX. That all men have a natural and unalienable right to worship Almighty God according to the dictates of their own consciences.

Constitution

XXXIV. That there shall be no establishment of any one religious church or denomination in this State, in preference to any other; neither shall any person, on any pretence whatsoever, be compelled to attend any place of worship contrary to his own faith or judgment, nor be obliged to pay, for the purchase of any glebe, or the building of any house of worship, or for the maintenance of any minister or ministry, contrary to what he believes right, or has voluntarily and personally engaged to perform; but all persons shall be at liberty to exercise their own mode of worship:—*Provided*, That nothing herein contained shall be construed to exempt preachers of treasonable or seditious discourses, from legal trial and punishment.

Vermont Constitution, *July 8, 1777*

Declaration of Rights

III. That all men have a natural and unalienable right to worship ALMIGHTY GOD, according to the dictates of their own

---

2. Plots of land belonging to churches.

consciences and understanding, regulated by the word of GOD; and that no man ought, or of right can be compelled to attend any religious worship, or erect, or support any place of worship, or maintain any minister, contrary to the dictates of his conscience; nor can any man who professes the protestant religion, be justly deprived or abridged of any civil right, as a citizen, on account of his religious sentiment, or peculiar mode of religious worship, and that no authority can, or ought to be vested in, or assumed by, any power whatsoever, that shall, in any case, interfere with, or in any manner controul, the rights of conscience, in the free exercise of religious worship: nevertheless, every sect or denomination of people ought to observe the Sabbath, or the Lord's day, and keep up, and support, some sort of religious worship, which to them shall seem most agreeable to the revealed will of GOD.

Plan or Frame of Government

SECTION VI. Every man of the full age of twenty-one years, having resided in this State for the space of one whole year, next before the election of representatives, and who is of a quiet and peaceable behaviour, and will take the following oath (or affirmation) shall be entitled to all the privileges of a freeman of this State.

I ____ ____ solemnly swear, by the ever living God, (or affirm, in the presence of Almighty God,) that whenever I am called to give my vote or suffrage, touching any matter that concerns the State of Vermont, I will do it so, as in my conscience, I shall judge will most conduce to the best good of the same, as established by the constitution, without fear or favor of any man.

SECTION IX. A quorum of the house of representatives shall consist of two-thirds of the whole number of members elected; and having met and chosen their speaker, shall, each of them, before they proceed to business, take and subscribe, as well the oath of fidelity and allegiance herein after directed, as the following oath or affirmation, viz.

"I _____ _____ do solemnly swear, by the ever living God, (or, I do solemnly affirm in the presence of Almighty God) that as a member of this assembly, I will not propose or assent to any bill, vote, or resolution, which shall appear to me injurious to the people; nor do or consent to any act or thing whatever, that shall have a tendency to lessen or abridge their rights and privileges, as declared in the Constitution of this State; but will, in all things conduct myself as a faithful, honest representative and guardian of the people, according to the best of my judgment and abilities."

And each member, before he takes his seat, shall make and subscribe the following declaration, viz.

"I do believe in one God, the Creator and Governor of the universe, the rewarder of the good and punisher of the wicked. And I do acknowledge the scriptures of the old and new testament to be given by divine inspiration, and own and profess the protestant religion."

And no further or other religious test shall ever, hereafter, be required of any civil officer or magistrate in this State.

Maryland Constitution, *November 11, 1776*

XXXIII. That, as it is the duty of every man to worship God in such manner as he thinks most acceptable to him; all persons, professing the Christian religion, are equally entitled to protection in their religious liberty; wherefore no person ought by any law to be molested in his person or estate on account of his religious persuasion or profession, or for his religious practice; unless, under colour of religion, any man shall disturb the good order, peace or safety of the State, or shall infringe the laws of morality, or injure others, in their natural, civil, or religious rights; nor ought any person to be compelled to frequent or maintain, or contribute, unless on contract, to maintain any particular place of worship, or any particular ministry; yet the Legislature may, in their discretion, lay a general and equal tax, for the support of the Christian religion; leaving to each individual the power of appointing the payment over of the money, collected from him, to the support of any particular place of worship or minister, or for the benefit of the poor of his own denomination, or the poor in general of any particular county: but the churches, chapels, glebes, and all other property now belonging to the church of England, ought to remain to the church of England forever . . .

XXXV. That no other test or qualification ought to be required, on admission to any office of trust or profit, than such oath of support and fidelity to this State, and such oath of office, as shall be directed by this Convention, or the Legislature of this State, and a declaration of a belief in the Christian religion.

XXXVI. That the manner of administering an oath to any person, ought to be such, as those of the religious persuasion, profession, or denomination, of which such person is one, generally esteem the most effectual confirmation, by the attestation of the Divine Being. And that the people called Quakers, those called Dunkers, and those called Menonists,[3] holding it unlawful to take an oath on any occasion, ought to be allowed to make their solemn affirmation, in the manner that Quakers have been heretofore allowed to affirm; and to be of the same avail as an oath, in all such cases, as the affirmation of Quakers hath

3. Mennonites, or German Anabaptists.

been allowed and accepted within this State, instead of an oath. And further, on such affirmation, warrants to search for stolen goods, or for the apprehension or commitment of offenders, ought to be granted, or security for the peace awarded, and Quakers, Dunkers or Menonists ought also, on their solemn affirmation as aforesaid, to be admitted as witnesses, in all criminal cases not capital.

2. ISAAC BACKUS ARGUES FOR RELIGIOUS FREEDOM, 1773

After his conversion in the Great Awakening, Isaac Backus separated from the established Congregational church in his hometown of Norwich, Connecticut, and later became a Baptist. As a Separate and a Baptist, Backus and his family suffered persecution from the governments of Connecticut and Massachusetts. He became not only the key Baptist organizer in New England, but also the chief opponent of Massachusetts's established church. In this pamphlet from 1773, he called for full religious freedom and compared the evangelical dissenters' cause to the colonists' argument for freedom from British taxes.

From Isaac Backus, *An Appeal to the Public for Religious Liberty* (Boston, 1773), 52–60.

The great importance of a general union through this country, in order to the preservation of our liberties, has often been pleaded for with propriety; but how can such a union be expected so long as that dearest of all rights, equal liberty of conscience is not allowed? Yea, how can any reasonably expect that he who has the hearts of kings in his hand, will turn the heart of our earthly sovereign to hear the pleas for liberty, of those who will not hear the cries of their fellow-subjects, under their oppressions? Has it not been plainly proved, that so far as any man gratifies his own inclinations, without regard to the universal law of equity, so far he is in bondage? so that it is impossible for any one to tyranize over others, without thereby becoming a miserable slave himself: a slave to raging lusts, and a slave to guilty fears of what will be the consequence....

Suffer us a little to expostulate with our fathers and brethren, who inhabit the land to which our ancestors fled for religious liberty. You have lately been accused with being disorderly and rebellious, by men in power, who profess a great regard for order and the public good; and why don't you believe them, and rest easy under their administrations? You tell us you cannot, because you are taxed where you are not represented; and is it not really so with us? You do not deny the right of the British parliament to impose taxes within her own realm; only complain that she extends her taxing power beyond her proper limits; and have we not as good right to say you do the *same thing*? and so that wherein you judge others you condemn your selves? Can three thousand miles possibly fix such limits to taxing power, as the difference between civil and sacred matters has already done? One is only a distance of *space*, the other is so great a difference in the *nature* of things, as there is between *sacrifices to God*, and the *ordinances of men*. This we trust has been fully proved.

If we ask why have you not been easy and thankful since the parliament has taken off so many of the taxes that they had laid upon us? you answer that they still claim a power to tax us, when, and as much as they please; and is not that the very difficulty before us?...

Many think it hard to be frowned upon only for pleading for their rights, and laying open particular acts of encroachment thereon; but what frowns have we met with for no other crime? and as the present contest between Great-Britain and America, is not so much about the greatness of the taxes already laid, as about a submission to their taxing power; so (though what we have already suffered is far from being a trifle, yet) our greatest difficulty at present concerns the submitting to a taxing power in ecclesiastical affairs. It is supposed by many that we are exempted from such taxes, but they are greatly mistaken, for all know that paper is a money article, and writing upon it is labour, and this tax we must pay every year, as a token of submission to their power, or else they will lay a heavier tax upon us. And we have one difficulty in submitting to this power, which our countrymen have not in the other case: that is, our case affects the conscience, as theirs does not: and equal liberty of conscience is one essential article in our CHARTER, which constitutes this government, and describes the extent of our rulers authority, and what are the rights and liberties of the people. And in the confession of faith[4] which our rulers and their ministers have published to the world, they say, "God alone is Lord of the conscience, and hath left it free from the doctrines and commandments of men, which are, in *any thing* contrary to his word; or *not contained in it*; so that to believe such doctrines, or to obey such commands, out of conscience, is to *betray* true liberty of conscience; and the requiring of an implicit faith, and an absolute blind obedience, is to destroy liberty of conscience and reason also." . . .

[I]f the constitution of this government, gives the magistrate no other authority than what belongs to *civil society*, we desire to

4. The Westminster Confession of Faith (1646).

know how he ever came to *impose* any particular *way of worship*, upon any town or precinct whatsoever? And if a man has a right to his *estate*, his *liberty* and his *family*, notwithstanding his non-conformity to the magistrate's way of worship, by what authority has any man had his goods spoiled, his land sold, or his person imprisoned, and thereby deprived of the enjoyment both of his liberty and his family, for no crime at all against the peace or welfare of the state, but only because he refused to conform to, or to support an *imposed* way of worship, or an *imposed* minister . . .

Thus we have laid before the public a brief view of our sentiments concerning liberty of conscience, and a little sketch of our sufferings on that account. If any can show us that we have made any mistakes, either about principles or facts, we would lie open to conviction: But we hope none will violate the forecited article of faith so much, as to require us to yield a *blind obedience* to them, or to expect that spoiling of goods or imprisonment can move us to *betray* the cause of true liberty . . .

3. MASSACHUSETTS CONSTITUTION OF 1780

In 1780, Massachusetts adopted a new constitution with an endorsement of religious freedom, but a continuation of its Congregationalist established church. Article III of the Declaration of Rights provided for the tax support of "public Protestant teachers of piety, religion, and morality." In spite of pressure from evangelical Baptists and liberal Christians, Massachusetts did not drop its establishment of religion until 1833.

From Thorpe, ed., *Federal and State Constitutions*, 3:1889–1890.

[Declaration of Rights]

Art. II. It is the right as well as the duty of all men in society, publicly, and at stated seasons, to worship the Supreme Being, the great Creator and Preserver of the universe. And no subject shall be hurt, molested, or restrained, in his person, liberty, or estate, for worshipping God in the manner and season most agreeable to the dictates of his own conscience; or for his religious profession of sentiments; provided he doth not disturb the public peace, or obstruct others in their religious worship.

Art. III. As the happiness of a people, and the good order and preservation of civil government, essentially depend upon piety, religion, and morality; and as these cannot be generally diffused through a community but by the institution of the public worship of God, and of public instructions in piety, religion, and morality: Therefore, to promote their happiness, and to secure the good order and preservation of their government, the people of this commonwealth have a right to invest their legislature with power to authorize and require, and the legislature shall, from time to time, authorize and require, the several towns, parishes, precincts, and other bodies politic, or religious societies, to make suitable provision, at their own expense, for the institution of the public worship of God and for the support and maintenance of public Protestant teachers of piety, religion, and morality, in all cases where such provision shall not be made voluntarily.

And the people of this commonwealth have also a right to, and do, invest their legislature with authority to enjoin upon all the subjects an attendance upon the instructions of the public teachers aforesaid, at stated times and seasons, if there be any on whose instructions they can conscientiously and conveniently attend.

Provided, notwithstanding, that the several towns, parishes, precincts, and other bodies politic, or religious societies, shall, at all times, have the exclusive right of electing their public teachers, and of contracting with them for their support and maintenance.

And all moneys paid by the subject to the support of public worship, and of the public teachers aforesaid, shall, if he require it, be uniformly applied to the support of the public teacher or teachers of his own religious sect or denomination, provided there be any on whose instructions he attends; otherwise it may be paid toward the support of the teacher or teachers of the parish or precinct in which the said moneys are raised.

And every denomination of Christians, demeaning themselves peaceably, and as good subjects of the commonwealth, shall be equally under the protection of the law: and no subordination of any one sect or denomination to another shall ever be established by law.

4. BOSTON SUPPORTS THE ESTABLISHMENT, 1780

Article III of the Declaration of Rights in the Massachusetts Constitution proved to be highly controversial. As reflected in this document from the Boston town records of 1780, many in Massachusetts wished to preserve the establishment in order to promote public morality. They did not see a contradiction between public support for religion, and religious freedom.

From *A Report of the Record Commissioners of the City of Boston* (Boston, 1895), 134.

The only Article now to be attended to is the third in the Deceleration of Rights, which Asserts that Piety, Religion and morality are essential to the happiness, Peace and Good order of a People and that these Principles are diffused by the Publick

Worship of God, and by Publick Instructions [etc.]—and in Consequence makes provision for their support. The alterations proposed here which you will Lay before the Convention were designed to Secure the Reights of Consience and to give the fullest Scope to religious Liberty[.] In support of the proposition it urged that if Publick Worship and Publick teaching, did certainly (as was allowed) defuse a general Sence of Duty & moral Obligations, and, so secured the safety of our Persons and Properties, we ought chearfully to pay those from whose agency we derived such Advantages. But we are Attempting to support (it is said) the Kingdom of Christ; It may as well be said we are supporting the Kingdom of God, by institution of a Civil Goverment, which Declared to be an Ordinance to the Deity, and so refuse to pay the civil magistrate. What will be the consequence of such refusal—The greatest disorders, if not a Dissolution of Society. Suspend all provision for the inculation of Morality, religion and Piety, and confusion & every evil work may be justly dreaded; for it is found that with all the Restraints of religion induced by the Preaching of Ministers, and with all the Restraints of Goverment inforced by civil Law, the World is far from being as quiet an abode as might be wished. Remove the former by ceasing to support Morality, religion and Piety and it will be soon felt that human Laws were feble barriers opposed to the uninformed lusts of Passions of Mankind. But though we are not supporting the kingdom of Christ may we not be permitted to Assist civil society by an addoption, and by the teaching of the best set of Morals that were ever offered to the World. To Object to these Morrals, or even to the Piety and Religion we aim to inculcate, because they are drawn from the Gospel, must appear very singular to an Assembly generally professing themselves Christians. Were this really our intention, no Objection ought to be made to it provided, as in fact the case that equal Liberty is granted to every religious Sect and Denomination Whatever, and it is only required that every Man should pay to the support of Publick Worship In his own way. But should any be so Conscientious that they cannot pay to the support of any of the various denominations among us they may then alott their Money to the support of the Poor.

5. GRANVILLE, MASSACHUSETTS, OPPOSES THE ESTABLISHMENT, 1780

Granville, Massachusetts, overwhelmingly approved every portion of the Massachusetts Declaration of Rights except for Article III, which was almost unanimously opposed. Granville, in southwestern Massachusetts, was a hotbed of evangelical Baptists, who did not trust an intertwining of church and state. They had too much experience with persecution by the colonial governments and their state-sponsored churches. Granville's voters argued that there needed to be a clear distinction between the kingdom of Christ and the kingdoms of this world. Therefore, the state should not support any church financially.

From "The Struggle over the Adoption of the Constitution of Massachusetts, 1780," *Massachusetts Historical Society Proceedings* 50 (1916–1917): 406–407.

RETURN OF THE TOWN OF GRANVILLE ON ARTICLE III OF THE DECLARATION OF RIGHTS

The Objection to the third Article is as follows. The Article Asserts that the People have a Right to invest their Legislature with a Power to interfere in Matters that properly belong to the

Christian Church; after the most mature Consideration we are oblig'd to deny that any such Right is or can be invested in the Legislature; because.

1st Christ himself is the only Lord of Conscience & King & Law Giver in his Church. Teachers of Religion are Officers in his Kingdom, qualified & sent by him, for whose Maintenance he hath made sufficient Provision, by the Laws which belong to his own Kingdom. Therefore no supplementary Laws of human Legislatures are necessary.

2nd The interference of the Magistrate in Matters that belong to the Christian Church, is, in our View an Incroachment on the Kingly Office of Jesus Christ, who stands in no need of the help of any civil Legislature whatever; consequently is an Affront to him.

3rd The interference of the Civil Magistrate in Matters that belong to Christ & Conscience, ever has been, and ever will be productive of Oppression to Mankind. There could be no persecution if the civil Magistrate did not support the Power & Cruelty of Men of narrow & ambitious Minds.

4th True Religion has evidently declined & been currupted by the interference of Statesmen & Politicians. Church History proves this to have been the Case from the Days of Constantine[5] down to our own Day.

6. BENJAMIN FRANKLIN ON THE MASSACHUSETTS CONSTITUTION, 1780

Franklin, working as a diplomat in Paris, wrote to his friend Richard Price of London regarding the 1780 Massachusetts Constitution and its requirement that officers affirm a belief in the Christian religion,

5. The fourth-century CE Roman emperor who legalized Christianity and promoted its interests.

and its provision for state support of religion. A friend of a number of the leading American founders, Price was a Unitarian minister and philosopher who, like Franklin, opposed religious tests and state support for official denominations.

From Benjamin Franklin to Richard Price, October 9, 1780, in *The Papers of Benjamin Franklin*, ed. Barbara Oberg, 39 vols. (New Haven, CT, 1997), 33:389–390. Used by permission of the press.

I am fully of your Opinion respecting Religious Tests; but tho' the People of Massachusetts have not in their new Constitution kept quite clear of them; yet if we consider what that People were 100 Years ago, we must allow they have gone great Lengths in Liberality of Sentiment, on religious Subjects; and we may hope for greater Degrees of Perfection when their Constitution some years hence shall be revised. If Christian Preachers had continued to teach as Christ & his Apostles did, without Salaries, and as the Quakers now do, I imagine Tests would never have existed: For I think they were invented not so much to secure Religion itself, as the Emoluments of it.—When a Religion is good, I conceive that it will support itself; and when it cannot support itself, and God does not take care to support, so that its Professors are oblig'd to call for the help of the Civil Power, 'tis a Sign, I apprehend, of its being a bad one. But I shall be out of my Depth if I wade any deeper in Theology . . .

7. VIRGINIA DECLARATION OF RIGHTS, 1776

The new Virginia government endorsed the principle of the "free exercise of religion" in its Declaration of Rights. The state left the Episcopal church in place as the established denomination, however. This tension remained to be resolved in the 1780s, when the clash between religious establishment and religious freedom came to a head over Thomas Jefferson's Bill for Establishing Religious Freedom.

From Thorpe, ed., *Federal and State Constitutions*, 7:3814.

Virginia Constitution, *June 29, 1776*

Declaration of Rights

SEC. 16. That religion, or the duty which we owe to our Creator, and the manner of discharging it, can be directed only by reason and conviction, not by force or violence; and therefore all men are equally entitled to the free exercise of religion, according to the dictates of conscience; and that it is the mutual duty of all to practice Christian forbearance, love, and charity towards each other.

8. BILL FOR A GENERAL ASSESSMENT FOR RELIGION, 1784

At the beginning of the Revolutionary War, Virginia stopped funding the Episcopal church as a wartime exigency. In 1784, Patrick Henry introduced a bill to resume public funding for religion. Henry knew that the state would never return to a single established church, so he offered a plan known as a general assessment for religion. Under this system, Virginians would be required to pay taxes to support Protestant denominations, but they could choose which church would receive their contributions. The bill also made some concession to the Quakers and Mennonites in the state, who did not necessarily have paid ministers. Henry narrowly failed to pass the bill, partly because he left the legislature to become Virginia's governor in late 1784. James Madison, the bill's chief opponent, delayed a vote on the measure until 1785.

From *Virginia Journal and Alexandria Advertiser*, March 17, 1785.

A Bill for Establishing a Provision for Teachers of the Christian Religion.

Whereas the general diffusion of Christian knowledge hath a natural tendency to correct the morals of men, restrain their vices, and preserve the peace of society, which cannot be effected without a competent provision for learned teachers, who may be thereby enabled to devote their time and attention to the duty of instructing such citizens, as from their circumstances and want of education, cannot otherwise attain such knowledge; and it is judged that such provision may be made by the Legislature, without counteracting the liberal principle heretofore adopted and intended to be preserved by abolishing all distinctions of pre-eminence amongst the different societies or communities of Christians;

Be it therefore enacted by the General Assembly, That for the support of Christian teachers,—per centum on the amount, or—in the pound on the sum payable for tax on the property within this Commonwealth, is hereby assessed . . .

. . . the money to be raised by virtue of this act, shall be by the Vestries, Elders, or Directors of each religious society, appropriated to a provision for a Minister or Teacher of the Gospel of their denomination, or the providing place of divine worship, and to none other use whatsoever; except in the denominations of Quakers and Menonists, who may receive what is collected from their members, and place it in their general fund, to be disposed of in a manner which they shall think best calculated to promote their particular mode of worship.

9. JAMES MADISON, *MEMORIAL AND REMONSTRANCE*, 1785

Many Virginians stood against Henry's general assessment, especially Baptist evangelicals and liberal Episcopalians such as Madison. Almost a hundred petitions, primarily from evangelicals, opposed the assessment, because they believed that any state requirement of support for religion was a violation of the freedom of conscience. Madison's *Memorial and Remonstrance* was the most memorable attack on the assessment. He wrote this in 1785, after successfully delaying the vote on the general assessment. Madison argued that state support for religion not only contradicted Virginia's commitment to religious freedom, but it also hurt the interest of religion itself. Madison and the evangelicals' campaign was successful, and the general assessment bill was set aside in the legislature in 1785 due to a lack of support.

From *Letters and Other Writings of James Madison* (New York, 1884), 1:162–169.

To the Honorable the General Assembly of the Commonwealth of Virginia:

A MEMORIAL AND REMONSTRANCE.

We, the subscribers, citizens of the said Commonwealth, having taken into serious consideration a Bill printed by order of the last session of General Assembly, entitled "A Bill establishing a provision for Teachers of the Christian Religion," and conceiving that the same, if finally armed with the sanctions of a law, will be a dangerous abuse of power, are bound as faithful members of a free State to remonstrate against it, and to declare the reasons by which we are determined. We remonstrate against the said Bill—

1. Because we hold it for a fundamental and undeniable truth, "that Religion, or the duty which we owe to our Creator, and the manner of discharging it, can be directed only by reason and conviction, not by force or violence."[*] The Religion, then, of every man must be left to the conviction and conscience of every man; and it is the right of every man to exercise it, as these may dictate. This right is in its nature an unalienable right. It is unalienable, because the opinions of men, depending only on the evidence contemplated by their own minds, cannot follow the dictates of other men. It is unalienable, also, because what is here a right towards men is a duty towards the Creator. It is the duty of every man to render to the Creator such homage, and such only, as he believes to be acceptable to him. This duty is precedent, both in order of time and in degree of obligation, to the claims of Civil Society. Before any man can be considered as a member of Civil Society, he must be considered as a subject of the Governor of the Universe; and if a member of Civil Society who enters into any subordinate Association must always do it with a reservation of his duty to the General Authority, much more must every man who becomes a member of any particular Civil Society do it with a saving of his allegiance to the Universal Sovereign. We maintain, therefore, that in matters of Religion no man's right is abridged by the institution of Civil Society, and that Religion is wholly exempt from its cognizance. True it is, that no other rule exists by which any question which may divide

---

* [Madison's note:] Declaration [of] Rights, Article 16.

a Society can be ultimately determined than the will of the majority; but it is also true that the majority may trespass on the rights of the minority.

2. Because, if Religion be exempt from the authority of the Society at large, still less can it be subject to that of the Legislative Body. The latter are but the creatures and vicegerents of the former. Their jurisdiction is both derivative and limited. It is limited with regard to the co-ordinate departments; more necessarily is it limited with regard to the constituents. The preservation of a free Government requires, not merely that the metes and bounds which separate each department of power be invariably maintained, but more especially that neither of them be suffered to overleap the great Barrier which defends the rights of the people. The rulers who are guilty of such an encroachment exceed the commission from which they derive their authority, and are Tyrants. The people who submit to it are governed by laws made neither by themselves nor by an authority derived from them, and are slaves.

3. Because it is proper to take alarm at the first experiment on our liberties. We hold this prudent jealousy to be the first duty of citizens, and one of the noblest characteristics of the late Revolution. The freemen of America did not wait till usurped power had strengthened itself by exercise, and entangled the question in precedents. They saw all the consequences in the principle, and they avoided the consequences by denying the principle. We revere this lesson too much soon to forget it. Who does not see that the same authority which can establish Christianity, in exclusion of all other Religions, may establish, with the same ease, any particular sect of Christians, in exclusion of all other sects? That the same authority which can force a citizen to contribute three pence only of his property for the support of

any one establishment, may force him to conform to any other establishment in all cases whatsoever?

4. Because the Bill violates that equality which ought to be the basis of every law, and which is more indispensable in proportion as the validity or expediency of any law is more liable to be impeached. "If all men are by nature equally free and independent,"* all men are to be considered as entering into Society on equal conditions; as relinquishing no more, and therefore retaining no less, one than another, of their natural rights. Above all, are they to be considered as retaining an "equal title to the free exercise of Religion according to the dictates of conscience."[†] Whilst we assert for ourselves a freedom to embrace, to profess, and to observe, the Religion which we believe to be of divine origin, we cannot deny an equal freedom to them whose minds have not yet yielded to the evidence which has convinced us. If this freedom be abused, it is an offence against God, not against man. To God, therefore, not to man, must an account of it be rendered. As the bill violates equality by subjecting some to peculiar burdens, so it violates the same principle by granting to others peculiar exemptions. Are the Quakers and Menonists the only Sects who think a compulsive support of their Religions unnecessary and unwarrantable? Can their piety alone be entrusted with the care of public worship? Ought their Religions to be endowed above all others with extraordinary privileges, by which proselytes may be enticed from all others? We think too favourably of the justice and good sense of these denominations to believe that they either covet pre-eminences over their fellow-citizens, or that they will be seduced by them from the common opposition to the measure.

* Declaration [of] Rights, article 1.
† Article 16.

5. Because the Bill implies, either that the civil Magistrate is a competent Judge of Religious truths, or that he may employ Religion as an engine of civil policy. The first is an arrogant pretension, falsified by the contradictory opinions of Rulers in all ages, and throughout the world; the second, an unhallowed perversion of the means of salvation.

6. Because the establishment proposed by the Bill is not requisite for the support of the Christian Religion. To say that it is, is a contradiction to the Christian Religion itself, for every page of it disavows a dependence on the powers of this world. It is a contradiction to fact, for it is known that this Religion both existed and flourished, not only without the support of human laws, but in spite of every opposition from them; and not only during the period of miraculous aid, but long after it had been left to its own evidence and the ordinary care of providence. Nay, it is a contradiction in terms; for a Religion not invented by human policy must have pre-existed and been supported before it was established by human policy. It is, moreover, to weaken in those who profess this Religion a pious confidence in its innate excellence and the patronage of its Author; and to foster in those who still reject it a suspicion that its friends are too conscious of its fallacies to trust it to its own merits.

7. Because experience witnesseth that ecclesiastical establishments, instead of maintaining the purity and efficacy of Religion, have had a contrary operation. During almost fifteen Centuries has the legal establishment of Christianity been on trial. What have been its fruits? More or less, in all places, pride and indolence in the Clergy; ignorance and servility in the laity; in both, superstition, bigotry, and persecution. Enquire of the Teachers of Christianity for the ages in which it appeared in its greatest lustre; those of every Sect point to the ages prior to its

incorporation with civil policy. Propose a restoration of this primitive state, in which its Teachers depended on the voluntary rewards of their flocks; many of them predict its downfall. On which side ought their testimony to have greatest weight; when for or when against their interest?

8. Because the establishment in question is not necessary for the support of Civil Government. If it be urged as necessary for the support of Civil Government only as it is a means of supporting Religion, and it be not necessary for the latter purpose, it cannot be necessary for the former. If Religion be not within the cognizance of Civil Government, how can its legal establishment be necessary to Civil Government? What influence, in fact, have ecclesiastical establishments had on Civil Society? In some instances they have been seen to erect a spiritual tyranny on the ruins of the civil authority; in many instances they have been seen upholding the thrones of political tyranny; in no instance have they been seen the guardians of the liberties of the people. Rulers who wished to subvert the public liberty may have found an established Clergy convenient auxiliaries. A just Government, instituted to secure and perpetuate it, needs them not. Such a Government will be best supported by protecting every citizen in the enjoyment of his Religion with the same equal hand which protects his person and his property; by neither invading the equal rights of any Sect, nor suffering any sect to invade those of another.

9. Because the proposed establishment is a departure from that generous policy which, offering an Asylum to the persecuted and oppressed of every Nation and Religion, promised a lustre to our country, and an accession to the number of its citizens. What a melancholy mark is the Bill of sudden degeneracy! Instead of holding forth an Asylum to the persecuted, it is itself a

signal of persecution. It degrades from the equal rank of Citizens all those whose opinions in Religion do not bend to those of the Legislative authority. Distant as it may be in its present form from the Inquisition, it differs from it only in degree. The one is the first step, the other the last, in the career of intolerance. The magnanimous sufferer under this cruel scourge in foreign Regions must view the Bill as a Beacon on our Coast warning him to seek some other haven, where liberty and philanthropy, in their due extent, may offer a more certain repose from his troubles.

10. Because it will have a like tendency to banish our citizens. The allurements presented by other situations are every day thinning their number. To superadd a fresh motive to emigration by revoking the liberty which they now enjoy would be the same species of folly which has dishonoured and depopulated flourishing kingdoms.

11. Because it will destroy that moderation and harmony which the forbearance of our laws to intermeddle with Religion has produced among its several Sects. Torrents of blood have been spilt in the old world in consequence of vain attempts of the secular arm to extinguish Religious discord by proscribing all differences in Religious opinion. Time has at length revealed the true remedy. Every relaxation of narrow and rigorous policy, wherever it has been tried, has been found to assuage the disease. The American theatre has exhibited proofs that equal and complete liberty, if it does not wholly eradicate it, sufficiently destroys its malignant influence on the health and prosperity of the State. If, with the salutary effects of this system under our own eyes, we begin to contract the bounds of Religious freedom, we know no name which will too severely reproach our folly. At least, let warning be taken at the first fruits of the threatened innovation.

The very appearance of the Bill has transformed "that christian forbearance, love, and charity,"[*] which of late mutually prevailed, into animosities and jealousies, which may not soon be appeased. What mischiefs may not be dreaded, should this enemy to the public quiet be armed with the force of a law?

12. Because the policy of the Bill is adverse to the diffusion of the light of Christianity. The first wish of those who enjoy this precious gift ought to be, that it may be imparted to the whole race of mankind. Compare the number of those who have as yet received it with the number still remaining under the dominion of false Religions, and how small is the former! Does the policy of the Bill tend to lessen the disproportion? No; it at once discourages those who are strangers to the light of revelation from coming into the Region of it, and countenances by example the nations who continue in darkness in shutting out those who might convey it to them. Instead of levelling, as far as possible, every obstacle to the victorious progress of truth, the Bill, with an ignoble and unchristian timidity, would circumscribe it with a wall of defence against the encroachments of error.

13. Because attempts to enforce, by legal sanctions, acts obnoxious to so great a proportion of citizens, tend to enervate the laws in general, and to slacken the bands of Society. If it be difficult to execute any law which is not generally deemed necessary or salutary, what must be the case where it is deemed invalid and dangerous? And what may be the effect of so striking an example of impotency in the Government on its general authority?

14. Because a measure of such singular magnitude and delicacy ought not to be imposed without the clearest evidence that it is called for by a majority of citizens; and no satisfactory

* Declaration [of] Rights, Article 16.

method is yet proposed by which the voice of the majority in this case may be determined, or its influence secured. "The people of the respective Counties are, indeed, requested to signify their opinion respecting the adoption of the Bill to the next Session of the Assembly." But the representation must be made equal before the voice either of the Representatives or of the Counties will be that of the people. Our hope is, that neither of the former will, after due consideration, espouse the dangerous principle of the Bill. Should the event disappoint us, it will still leave us in full confidence that a fair appeal to the latter will reverse the sentence against our liberties.

15. Because, finally, "the equal right of every Citizen to the free exercise of his Religion, according to the dictates of conscience," is held by the same tenure with all our other rights. If we recur to its origin, it is equally the gift of nature; if we weigh its importance, it cannot be less dear to us; if we consult the Declaration of those rights "which pertain to the good people of Virginia as the basis and foundation of Government,"[*] it is enumerated with equal solemnity, or rather with studied emphasis. Either, then, we must say, that the will of the Legislature is the only measure of their authority, and that in the plenitude of that authority they may sweep away all our fundamental rights, or that they are bound to leave this particular right untouched and sacred. Either we must say, that they may controul the freedom of the press, may abolish the trial by jury, may swallow up the Executive and Judiciary powers of the State; nay, that they may despoil us of our very right of suffrage, and erect themselves into an independent and hereditary Assembly; or we must say, that they have no authority to enact into a law the Bill under consideration.

* Declaration [of] Rights, title.

We, the subscribers, say that the General Assembly of this Commonwealth have no such authority. And in order that no effort may be omitted on our part against so dangerous an usurpation, we oppose to it this remonstrance; earnestly praying, as we are in duty bound, that the Supreme Lawgiver of the Universe, by illuminating those to whom it is addressed, may, on the one hand, turn their councils from every act which would affront his holy prerogative, or violate the trust committed to them; and on the other, guide them into every measure which may be worthy of his blessing, redound to their own praise, and establish more firmly the liberties, the prosperity, and the happiness of the Commonwealth.

10. BILL FOR ESTABLISHING RELIGIOUS FREEDOM, 1786

With the defeat of Henry's general assessment, the path was open for Thomas Jefferson's Bill for Establishing Religious Freedom. Jefferson had originally drafted this bill in 1779, but it lacked sufficient support until 1786. By then, Jefferson had already begun serving as American diplomatic minister to Paris, but his close ally James Madison took up the cause of religious freedom in his absence. The bill represented one of Jefferson's most inspired writings, with its passionate case for liberty of conscience. The statute prohibited state support for any church and civil penalties for religious beliefs. It adopted a remarkably modern form of church-state separation. The bill was a critical precedent for the religion clauses of the First Amendment to the Constitution (1791), which banned a national establishment of religion, and guaranteed Americans "free exercise" of religion. The Virginia statute made Jefferson a hero of many evangelicals in America, despite his unorthodox religious beliefs. Jefferson listed this bill as one of only three accomplishments on his tombstone, along with writing the Declaration of Independence and founding the University of Virginia.

From the *Pennsylvania Evening Herald*, February 4, 1786. [The legislature slightly shortened the original version of Jefferson's bill, but the following text was adopted and publicized at the time.] An Act for Establishing Religious Freedom.

Whereas Almighty God hath created the mind free; that all attempts to influence it by temporal punishments or burdens, or by civil incapacitations, tend only to beget habits of hypocrisy and meanness, and are a departure from the plan of the Holy Author of our religion, who, being Lord both of body and mind, yet chose not to propagate it by coercions on either, as was in his Almighty power to do; that the impious presumption of legislators and rulers, civil as well as ecclesiastical, who, being themselves but fallible and uninspired men, have assumed dominion over the faith of others, setting up their own opinions and modes of thinking as the only true and infallible, and as such endeavoring to impose them on others, have established and maintained false religions over the greatest part of the world, and through all time: That to compel a man to furnish contributions of money for the propagation of opinions which he disbelieves, is sinful and tyrannical; that even the forcing him to support this or that preacher of his own religious persuasion, is depriving him of the comfortable liberty of giving his contributions to the particular pastor whose morals he would make his pattern, and whose powers he feels most persuasive to righteousness, and is withdrawing from the ministry those temporary rewards, which, proceeding from an approbation of their personal conduct, are an additional excitement to earnest and unremitting labours for the instruction of mankind; that our civil rights have no dependence on our religious opinions, any more than our opinions in physic or geometry; that therefore the proscribing any citizen, as unworthy the public confidence, by laying upon him an incapacity of being called to offices of trust or emolument, unless he profess or renounce this or that religious opinion, is depriving him injudiciously of those privileges and advantages, to which, in common with his fellow citizens, he has a natural right; that it tends only to corrupt the principles of that very religion it is meant to encourage, by bribing, with a monopoly of worldly honours and emoluments, those who will externally profess and conform to it; that though indeed those are criminal who do not withstand such temptation, yet neither are those innocent who lay the bait in their way; that to suffer the civil magistrate to intrude his powers into the field of opinion, and to restrain the profession or propagation of principles, on supposition of their ill tendency, is a dangerous fallacy, because he being of course judge of that tendency, will make his opinions the rule of judgment, and approve or condemn the sentiments of others, only as they shall square with, or differ from, his own; that it is time enough, for the rightful purposes of civil government, for its officers to interfere, when principles break out into overt acts against peace and good order; and finally, that truth is great, and will prevail, if left to herself; that she is the proper and sufficient antagonist to error, and has nothing to fear from the conflict, unless by human interposition disarmed of her natural weapons, free argument and debate, errors ceasing to be dangerous when it is permitted freely to contradict them:

Be it therefore enacted, [etc.] That no man shall be compelled to frequent or support any religious worship, place, or minister whatsoever, nor shall he be enforced, restrained, molested, or burdened in his body or goods, nor shall otherwise suffer on account of his religious opinions or belief; but that all men shall be free to profess, and by argument to maintain their opinions in matters of religion, and that the same shall in no wise diminish, enlarge, or affect their civil capacities.

And though we well know that this assembly, elected by the people for the ordinary purposes of legislation only, have no power to restrain the acts of succeeding assemblies, constituted with powers equal to our own, and that therefore to declare this act irrevocable, would be of no effect in law, yet we are free to declare, that the rights hereby asserted, are of the natural rights of mankind, and that if any act shall be hereafter passed to repeal the present, or to narrow its operation, such act will be an infringement of natural right.

11. CRITICISM OF THE BILL FOR ESTABLISHING RELIGIOUS FREEDOM, 1786

Despite its passage, many Americans saw Jefferson's Bill for Establishing Religious Freedom as an attack on Christianity. This writer from Pennsylvania believed that Jefferson's kind of church-state separation would open the door for non-Christians, including atheists and Muslims, to gain political office. He commended Pennsylvania's system, which maintained an oath for politicians affirming a belief in God and the Old and New Testaments. Following the growing trend toward religious freedom, however, Pennsylvania instituted a more general oath of belief in God in 1790. This profession would have still excluded atheists, but it included religious groups such as Jews as potential officeholders.

From John Swanwick, *Considerations on an Act of the Legislature of Virginia, Entitled An Act for the Establishment of Religious Freedom* (Philadelphia, 1786), iii–iv.

To the Reverend Clergy of all Christian denominations in the City of Philadelphia, and to the Public Friends of the respectable Society called Quakers, in this Metropolis.

Gentlemen,

The following sheets contain a few hasty reflections drawn up in short intervals of leisure, as they occurred to my mind on the perusal of the annexed act of assembly, lately passed by the state of Virginia, entitled, "An act for the establishment of religious freedom;" which, considering the tolerating spirit prevailing all over America, I was led to consider as unnecessary; but which, if the objects of it were even of such a nature as to require to be fixed by a permanent law, still will leave this act justly liable to many objections, both on account of the erroneous reasoning it contains, and its being more a general declamation against all religion, than an attempt to fix the freedom of any on a liberal and just foundation. By this act you will see, I am sure, not without regret, that a door is opened wide for the introduction of any tenets in religion, however degrading to christianity, or however tending to its destruction; that all countenance or support of government to it is withdrawn, and that the legislature of Virginia may be held and administ[e]red by men professedly atheists, Mahometans, or of any other creed, however unfriendly to liberty or the morals of a free country.

When you consider this, Gentlemen, I am sure you will feel with me one motive more of attachment to Pennsylvania, where the important concerns of religion are not so lightly esteemed; being thought worthy of the protection of its constitution, in which a pledge of security to the christian faith hath been interwoven with its political sanctions; and this is merited by the most amiable and pacific temper prevailing among the religious of all denominations in this state; a disposition which it is your study on all occasions to cultivate, as it is by your venerable and exemplary lives to give the fullest refutation to all the calumnies and invectives usually applied to the profession of piety by the prophane.

12. AN ACT FOR SUPPRESSING VICE AND IMMORALITY IN MARYLAND, 1786

After the War for Independence ended in 1783, many state legislatures passed laws prohibiting work on the Sabbath, taking the Lord's name in vain, and other practices deemed unholy and impure. This act, passed by the Maryland legislature, called for hefty fines to citizens who committed acts of "vice and immorality."

From the *Maryland Gazette*, February 2, 1786.
A bill, entitled An ACT for the suppression of vice and immorality.
Be it enacted, by the General Assembly of Maryland,
That if any free white person, after the commencement of this act, shall do any bodily labour, or, being a tradesman, shall work in his trade or business on the Lord's day, commonly called Sunday, or any part thereof (that is, between twelve o'clock on Saturday night, and the same hour on Sunday night, works of necessity or charity excepted), such person shall forfeit twenty shillings current money for every offense.

And be it enacted, That if any owner of any slave, servant, or apprentice, shall command or direct any such slave, servant, or apprentice, to do any manner of bodily work or labour (works of necessity and charity only excepted) on the Lord's day, he shall forfeit twenty shillings current money for every offense; and if the owner of any slave, servant, or apprentice, to do any manner of bodily work or labour (except from necessity) on the Lord's day, or to profane the said day by swearing or doing business, or by cock-fighting or other pastimes or recreations, or by fishing, fowling, or hunting, such owner shall forfeit ten shillings current money for every offence. . . .

An ACT to punish blasphemers, swearers, drunkards, and Sabbath-breakers; and for repealing the laws heretofore made for the punishing such offenders.

Be it enacted, by the right honourable the lord proprietor,[6] *by and with the advice and consent of his lordship's governor, and the upper and lower houses of assembly, and the authority of the same,* That if any person shall hereafter, within this province, wittingly, maliciously, and advisedly, by writing or speaking blaspheme or curse GOD, or deny our Saviour JESUS CHRIST to be the son of GOD, or shall deny the Holy Trinity, the Father, Son, and Holy Ghost, or the Godhead of any of the Three Persons, or the Unity of the Godhead, or shall utter any profane words concerning the Holy Trinity, or any of the persons thereof, and shall be [convicted] by verdict, or confession, shall, for the said offense be bored through the tongue, and fined twenty pounds sterling to the lord proprietor. . . .

---

6. Gubernatorial title for the governors of the former proprietary colonies. Maryland, North Carolina, and New Jersey were all proprietary colonies.

Chapter 3

Constitution and Ratification

1. BENJAMIN FRANKLIN'S PRAYER REQUEST AT THE CONSTITUTIONAL CONVENTION—AND THE RESPONSE, 1787

In the summer of 1787 fifty-five delegates from twelve of the thirteen states met in Philadelphia to revise the Articles of Confederation. Almost immediately, however, regional and ideological issues emerged, which threatened the stability of the Convention. Small states' delegates wanted to revise the Articles; large states' delegates wanted to scrap them altogether and start anew. Once it was decided to write a new constitution, delegates clashed over a variety of issues, the most important of which were slavery, representation in the House and Senate, and the presidency. Representation was a particularly thorny issue, as large states favored a bicameral legislature with proportional representation in both the House and the Senate, while small states supported a unicameral legislature in which each state, regardless of size, would have an equal vote. The discussions became so intense that midway through the Convention several delegates threatened to leave. It was "during that period of gloom," delegate James Madison later recalled, that Benjamin Franklin of Pennsylvania proposed that delegates pray, asking God to guide them in their deliberations. Madison's notes are not clear why the delegates rebuffed Franklin's request, but later Alexander Hamilton, one of the youngest delegates at the Convention, said that "he did not see the necessity of calling [o]n foreign aid."

From Max Farrand, ed., *The Records of the Federal Convention of 1787*, 4 vols. (New Haven, CT, 1911), 1:450–452.

Thursday, June 28, 1787

Mr. President:[1]

The small progress we have made after 4 or five weeks close attendance & continual reasonings with each other—our different sentiments on almost every question, several of the last producing as many noes as ays, is methinks a melancholy proof of the imperfection of the Human Understanding. We indeed seem to feel our own want of political wisdom, since we have been running about in search of it. We have gone back to ancient history for models of Government, and examined the different forms of those Republics which having been formed with the seeds of their own dissolution now no longer exist. And we have viewed Modern States all round Europe, but find none of their Constitutions suitable to our circumstances.

In this situation of this Assembly, groping as it were in the dark to find political truth, and scarce able to distinguish it when presented to us, how has it happened, Sir, that we have not hitherto once thought of humbly applying to the Father of lights to illuminate our understandings? In the beginning of the Contest with G. Britain, when we were sensible of danger we had daily prayer in this room for the divine protection.[2]—Our prayers, Sir, were heard, and they were graciously answered. All of us who

1. Refers to the president of the Convention, George Washington.
2. Delegates at the Continental Congress frequently prayed as they discussed the war effort against Great Britain.

were engaged in the struggle must have observed frequent instances of a Superintending providence in our favor. To that kind providence we owe this happy opportunity of consulting in peace on the means of establishing our future national felicity. And have we now forgotten that powerful friend? or do we imagine that we no longer need his assistance?

I have lived, Sir, a long time, and the longer I live, the more convincing proofs I see of this truth—*that God governs in the affairs of men.* And if a sparrow cannot fall to the ground without his notice, is it probable that an empire can rise without his aid? We have been assured, Sir, in the sacred writings that "except the Lord build the House they labour in vain that build it." I firmly believe this; and I also believe that without his concurring aid we shall succeed in this political building no better than the Builders of Babel:[3] We shall be divided by our little partial local interests; our projects will be confounded, and we ourselves shall become a reproach and bye word down to future ages. And what is worse, mankind may hereafter from this unfortunate instance, despair of establishing Governments by Human Wisdom and leave it to chance, war and conquest.

I therefore beg leave to move—that henceforth prayers imploring the assistance of Heaven, and its blessings on our deliberations, be held in this Assembly every morning before we proceed to business, and that one or more of the Clergy of this City be requested to officiate in that service.

Mr. Sherman[4] seconded the motion.

Mr. Hamilton[5] & several others expressed their apprehensions that however proper such a resolution might have been at

---

3. Refers to the Tower of Babel in the Old Testament.
4. Roger Sherman of Connecticut.
5. Alexander Hamilton of New York.

the beginning of the convention, it might at this late day, 1. bring on it some disagreeable animadversions.[6] & 2. lead the public to believe that the embarrassments and dissentions within the convention, had suggested this measure. It was answered by Docr. F.[7] Mr. Sherman & others, that the past omission of a duty could not justify a further omission—that the rejection of such a proposition would expose the Convention to more unpleasant animadversions than the adoption of it: and that the alarm out of doors that might be excited for the state of things within. Would at least be as likely to do good as ill.

Mr. Williamson,[8] observed that the true cause of the omission could not be mistaken. The Convention had no funds.

Mr. Randolph[9] proposed in order to give a favorable aspect to [the] measure, that a sermon be preached at the request of the convention on 4th of July, the anniversary of Independence,—& thenceforward prayers be used in [the] Convention every morning. Dr. Franklin 2ded. this motion After several unsuccessful attempts for silently postponing the matter by adjourn[in]g. The adjournment was at length carried, without any vote on the motion.

2. LUTHER MARTIN QUESTIONS WHY THERE IS NO RELIGIOUS OATH IN THE CONSTITUTION, 1787

The delegates at the First and Second Continental Congresses frequently invoked God's name in their state papers, speeches, and public proclamations. Perusing them reads like a script from

6. Strong criticism.
7. Benjamin Franklin of Pennsylvania.
8. Hugh Williamson of North Carolina.
9. Edmund Randolph of Virginia.

the Bible. Phrases like "Almighty God," "Providence," "Creator," "Lord of Hosts," "Nature's God," and "Jesus Christ" all gave religious sanction to what they were doing. Yet compared to the Declaration of Independence, the state constitutions of the 1770s, and the Articles of Confederation of 1781, the framework of government the Founders created in 1787 is surprisingly secular. It contains no acknowledgement of God, Jesus, or the most prominent idiom of the day, Providence. The only references delegates made to religion was in article 1, emphasizing that the president should not sign bills on Sunday; article 6, forbidding religious oaths as a qualification for public office; and article 7, affirming that the Convention met in the "Year of our Lord one thousand and seven hundred and Eighty Seven." This critical statement by delegate Luther Martin of Maryland questions why there is no religious test in the Constitution, requiring officeholders to take an oath affirming allegiance to the Bible and to God.

From Luther Martin's Address to the Maryland Legislature, November 29, 1787, in *The Records of the Federal Convention of 1787*, ed. Max Farrand, 4 vols. (New Haven, CT, 1911), 3:227.

The part of the system which provides, that *no religious test* shall ever be required as a qualification to any office or public trust under the United States, was adopted by a great majority of the convention, and without much debate; however, there were some members *so unfashionable* as to think, that *a belief of the existence of a Deity*, and of a *state of future rewards and punishment* would be some security for the good conduct of our rulers, and that, in a Christian country, it would be *at least decent* to hold out some distinction between the professors of Christianity and downright infidelity or paganism.

3. WAS THE CONSTITUTION AN INSPIRED DOCUMENT?

George Washington believed the Constitution was an inspired document. He asserted that "Providence" had watched over the delegates' affairs during the Constitutional Convention and helped them establish a new framework of government. His friend and fellow Virginian, James Madison, echoed Washington's remarks, contending that it would be difficult for any man not to perceive God's influence over the nation's Founding. John Adams, on the other hand, disagreed. He thought it was absurd to suggest that God had inspired the framers of the Constitution any more than he would inspire the affairs of a common laborer.

From George Washington to Jonathan Trumbull, July 20, 1788, in *The Papers of George Washington: Presidential Series*, ed. W. W. Abbot and Dorothy Twohig, 15 vols. (Charlottesville, VA, 1987–), 6:389. Used by permission of the publisher. James Madison, *Federalist 37*, in *The Federalist on the New Constitution, Written in the Year 1788 by Mr. Hamilton, Mr. Madison, and Mr. Jay* (Hallowell, ME, 1831), 179; John Adams, *A Defence of the Constitutions of Government of the United States of America* (1787–1788), in *The Works of John Adams*, ed. Charles Francis Adams, 10 vols. (Boston, 1850–1856), 4:292.

George Washington, *1788*

Your friend Colonel Humphreys[10] informs me, from the wonderful revolution of sentiment in favor of federal measures, and the marvellous change for the better in the elections of your State, that he shall begin to suspect that miracles have not ceased.

10. David Humphreys was a colonel and aide to Washington during the American Revolution.

Indeed, for myself, since so much liberality has been displayed in the construction and adoption of the proposed general government, I am almost disposed to be of the same opinion. Or at least we may, with a kind of pious and grateful exultation, trace the finger of Providence through those dark and mysterious events, which first induced the States to appoint a general convention, and then led them one after another, by such steps as were best calculated to effect the object, into an adoption of the system recommended by that general convention; thereby in all human probability laying a lasting foundation for tranquillity and happiness, when we had but too much reason to fear, that confusion and misery were coming rapidly upon us. That the same good Providence may still continue to protect us, and prevent us from dashing the cup of national felicity just as it has been lifted to our lips, is the earnest prayer of, my dear Sir, your faithful friend,

James Madison, *1788*

Would it be wonderful if, under the pressure of all these difficulties, the convention should have been forced into some deviations from that artificial structure and regular symmetry, which an abstract view of the subject might lead an ingenious theorist to bestow on a constitution planned in his closet, or in his imagination? The real wonder is that so many difficulties should have been surmounted; and surmounted with an unanimity almost as unprecedented, as it must have been unexpected. It is impossible for any man of candour to reflect on this circumstance, without partaking of the astonishment. It is impossible, for the man of pious reflection, not to perceive in it a finger of that Almighty Hand, which has been so frequently and signally extended to our relief in the critical stages of the revolution—

John Adams, *1788*

The United States of America have exhibited, perhaps, the first example of governments erected on the simple principles of nature; and if men are now sufficiently enlightened to disabuse themselves of artifice, imposture, hypocrisy, and superstition, they will consider this event as an era in their history. Although the detail of the formation of the American governments is at present little known or regarded either in Europe or in America, it may hereafter become an object of curiosity. It will never be pretended that any persons employed in that service had interviews with the gods, or were in any degree under the inspiration of Heaven, more than those at work upon ships or houses, or laboring in merchandise or agriculture; it will forever be acknowledged that these governments were contrived merely by the use of reason and the senses . . .

4. JAMES MADISON AND PATRICK HENRY ON HUMAN NATURE, 1788

Two of the giants in Virginia politics—James Madison and Patrick Henry—vigorously debated the Constitution, both in print and in speeches they made during the ratification campaign. Formidable foes, they had different views of human nature, which affected the way they viewed the new Constitution. For Madison, humans were basically good even though they were not angels. Accordingly, he believed that a republican form of government would work because it had sufficient "controls" or checks and balances to prevent corruption in public office. Patrick Henry was not as optimistic. He likened the new Constitution to the debate over the Jay-Gardoqui Treaty in 1785–1786, in which northern states wanted to give Spain exclusive navigation rights to the Mississippi River for thirty years in exchange for shipping rights to Spain's West Indian and European seaports—a move that would benefit northern merchants at the expense of southerners. Henry saw this as clear evidence that, if given the chance, the northern states would act against the interest of the southern states. This would become much easier in the new Congress, where votes on treaties required only a simple majority to pass. Henry's southern allies defeated the Jay Treaty only because the Confederation Congress required a two-thirds majority on treaties. Henry believed that this episode confirmed his broader concern that Americans could never count on the innate benevolence of their rulers to act on behalf of all the people. The power of the national government had to be severely restrained, or it would become a tyrannical monster, just like the British government in the 1760s and 1770s.

From James Madison, *Federalist 51*, in *The Federalist on the New Constitution, Written in the Year 1788 by Mr. Hamilton, Mr. Madison, and Mr. Jay* (Hallowell, ME, 1831), 259; Patrick Henry, speech in the Virginia Ratifying Convention, June 12, 1788, in *The Debates in the Several State Conventions on the Adoption of the Federal Constitution*, ed. Jonathan Elliot, 4 vols. (Washington, DC, 1836), 3:325–327.

James Madison, 1788

But the great security against a gradual concentration of the several powers in the same department, consists in giving to those who administer each department, the necessary constitutional means, and personal motives, to resist encroachments of the others. The provision for defense must in this, as in all other cases, be made commensurate to the danger of attack. Ambition must be made to counteract ambition. The interest of the man must be connected with the constitutional rights of the place. It may be a reflection on human nature, that such devices should be necessary to control the abuses of government. But what is government itself, but the greatest of all reflections on human nature? If men were angels, no government would be necessary. If angels were to govern men, neither external nor internal controls on government would be necessary. In framing a government which is to be administered by men over men, the great difficulty lies in this: you must first enable the government to control the governed; and in the next place oblige it to control itself. A dependence on the people is, no doubt, the primary control on the government; but experience has taught mankind the necessity of auxiliary precautions.[11]

Patrick Henry, *1788*

As to the western country, notwithstanding our representation in Congress, and notwithstanding any regulation that may be made by Congress, it may be lost. The seven Northern States are determined to give up the Mississippi.[12] We are told that, in order to secure the navigation of the river, it was necessary to give it up, for twenty-five years, to the Spaniards, and that thereafter we should enjoy it forever, without any interruption from them. This argument resembles that which recommends adopting first and then amending. I think the reverse of what the honorable gentleman [Edmund Pendleton][13] said on the subject. Those seven states are decidedly against it. He tells us that it is the policy of the whole Union to retain it. If men were wise, virtuous, and honest, we might depend on an adherence to this policy.

11. Such as the power to impeach and remove corrupt leaders from office.
12. Mississippi River.
13. A Virginia politician, lawyer, and judge during the American Revolution.

Did we not know of the fallibility of human nature, we might rely on the present structure of this government. We might depend that the rules of propriety, and the general interest of the Union, would be observed. But the depraved nature of man is well known. He has a natural bias towards his own interest, which will prevail over every consideration, unless it be checked.

The Northern States will never assent to regulations promotive of southern aggrandizement.[14] Notwithstanding what gentlemen say of the probable virtue of our representatives, I dread the depravity of human nature. I wish to guard against it by proper checks, and trust nothing to accident or chance. I will never depend on so slender a protection as the possibility of being represented by virtuous men.

5. OLIVER ELLSWORTH AND WILLIAM WILLIAMS DEBATE THE ABSENCE OF A RELIGIOUS OATH IN THE CONSTITUTION, 1787–1788

When some Anti-Federalists read the Constitution for the first time, they were angry that it did not contain a declaration of Protestant Christianity, an acknowledgment of God or Jesus, or a statement affirming the "Great Governor of the World," as the Articles of Confederation, America's first constitution, did. Furthermore, they were troubled that the framers rejected the common practice in the state constitutions requiring religious oaths for public office. This omission, they complained, would open the door for non-Christians to serve in government, thus betraying America's Christian heritage. Consequently, some critics like William Williams, a

---

14. Promoting or supporting southern commerce.

prominent merchant and delegate to the state ratification convention in Connecticut, wanted to amend the Constitution and acknowledge America's religious heritage by adding a religious oath. Others, such as Oliver Ellsworth, a delegate from Connecticut at both the Constitutional Convention and the state ratifying convention, rejected the idea. He believed that religious oaths violated the principles of religious liberty.

From [Oliver Ellsworth], "A Landholder" VII, *Connecticut Courant*, December 17, 1787; William Williams to the Printer, *American Mercury*, February 11, 1788.

Oliver Ellsworth, *December 17, 1787*

Some very worthy persons, who have not had great advantages for information, have objected against that clause in the constitution, which provides, that *no religious test shall ever be required as a qualification to any office or public trust under the United States.* They have been afraid that this clause is unfavourable to religion. But, my countrymen, the sole purpose and effect of it is to exclude persecution, and to secure to you the important right of religious liberty. We are almost the only people in the world, who have a full enjoyment of this important right of human nature. In our country every man has a right to worship God in that way which is most agreeable to his own conscience. If he be a good and peaceable citizen, he is liable to no penalties or incapacities on account of his religious sentiments; or in other words, he is not subject to persecution.

But in other parts of the world, it has been, and still is, far different. Systems of religious error have been adopted, in times of ignorance. It has been the interest of tyrannical kings, popes, and prelates,[15] to maintain these errors. When the clouds of ignorance began to vanish, and the people grew more enlightened, there was no other way to keep them in error, but to prohibit their altering their religious opinions by severe persecuting laws. In this way persecution became general throughout Europe. It was the universal opinion that one religion must be established by law; and that all, who differed in their religious opinions, must suffer the vengeance of persecution. In pursuance of this opinion, when popery[16] was abolished in England, and the church of England was established in its stead, severe penalties were inflicted upon all who dissented from the established church. In the time of the civil wars,[17] in the reign of Charles I, the presbyterians[18] got the upper hand, and inflicted legal penalties upon all who differed from them in their sentiments respecting religious doctrines and discipline. When Charles II, was restored, the church of England was likewise restored, and the presbyterians and other dissenters[19] were laid under legal penalties and incapacities. It was in this reign, that a religious test was established as a qualification for office; that is, a law was made requiring all officers civil and military (among other things) to receive the Sacrament of the Lord's Supper, according to the usage of the church of England, [within] six months after their admission to office, under the penalty of 500£[20] and disability to hold the office. And by another statute of the same reign, no person was capable of being elected to any office relating to the government

---

15. High-ranking church officers.
16. Catholicism.
17. English Civil Wars (1641–1651).
18. Presbyterians were supporters of Parliament during the English Civil Wars; they opposed an absolute monarchy.
19. Non-Anglicans, or those outside the Church of England.
20. Symbol for British currency, also known as the pound sign.

of any city or corporation, unless, within a twelvemonth before, he had received the Sacrament according to the rites of the church of England. The pretence for making these severe laws, by which all but churchmen were made incapable of any office civil or military, was to exclude the papists;[21] but the real design was to exclude the protestant dissenters. From this account of test-laws, there arises an unfavourable presumption against them. But if we consider the nature of them and the effects which they are calculated to produce, we shall find that they are useless, tyrannical, and peculiarly unfit for the people of this country.

A religious test is an act to be done, or profession to be made, relating to religion (such as partaking of the sacrament according to certain rites and forms, or declaring one's belief of certain doctrines,) for the purpose of determining, whether his religious opinions are such, that he is admissable to a public office. A test in favour of any one denomination of christians would be to the last degree absurd in the United States. If it were in favour of either congregationalists, presbyterians, episcopalions, baptists, or quakers; it would incapacitate more than three fourths of the American citizens for any public office; and thus degrade them from the rank of freemen. There needs no argument to prove that the majority of our citizens would never submit to this indignity.

If any test-act were to be made, perhaps the least exceptionable would be one, requiring all persons appointed to office, to declare, at the time of their admission, their belief in the being of a God, and in the divine authority of the scriptures. In favour of such a test, it may be said, that one who believes these great truths, will not be so likely to violate his obligations to his country, as one who disbelieves them; we may have greater confidence

---

21. Catholics.

in his integrity. But I answer: His making a declaration of such a belief is no security at all. For suppose him to be an unprincipled man, who believes neither the word nor the being of a God; and to be governed merely by selfish motives; how easy is it for him to dissemble? how easy is it for him to make a public declaration of his belief in the creed which the law prescribes; and excuse himself by calling it a mere formality? This is the case with the test-laws and creeds in England. The most abandoned characters partake of the sacrament, in order to qualify themselves for public employments. The clergy are obliged by law to administer the ordinance unto them; and thus prostitute the most sacred office of religion: for it is a civil right in the party to receive the sacrament. In that country, subscribing to the thirty-nine articles is a test for admission into holy orders. And it is a fact, that many of the clergy do this; when at the same time, they totally disbelieve several of the doctrines contained in them. In short, test-laws are utterly ineffectual; they are no security at all; because men of loose principles will, by an external compliance, evade them. If they exclude any persons, it will be honest men, men of principle, who will rather suffer an injury, than act contrary to the dictates of their consciences. If we mean to have those appointed to public offices, who are sincere friends to religion; we the people who appoint them, must take care to choose such characters; and not rely upon such cob-web barriers as test-laws are.

But to come to the true principle, by which this question ought to be determined: The business of a civil government is to protect the citizen in his rights, to defend the community from hostile powers, and to promote the general welfare. Civil government has no business to meddle with the private opinions of the people. If I demean myself as a good citizen, I am accountable, not to man, but to God, for the religious opinions which I embrace, and the manner in which I worship the supreme being. If such had been the universal sentiments of mankind, and they had acted accordingly, persecution, the bane of truth and nurse of error, with her bloody axe and flaming hand, would never have turned so great a part of the world into a field of blood.

But while I assert the right of religious liberty; I would not deny that the civil power has a right, in some cases, to interfere in matters of religion. It has a right to prohibit and punish gross immoralities and impieties; because the open practice of these is of evil example and public detriment. For this reason, I heartily approve of our laws against drunkenness, profane swearing, blasphemy, and professed atheism. But in this state, we have never thought it expedient to adopt a test-law; and yet I sincerely believe we have as great a proportion of religion and morality, as they have in England, where every person who holds a public office, must either be a saint by law, or a hypocrite by practice. A test-law is the parent of hypocrisy, and the offspring of error and the spirit of persecution. Legislatures have no right to set up an inquisition, and examine into the private opinions of men. Test-laws are useless and ineffectual, unjust and tyrannical; therefore the Convention have done wisely in excluding this engine of persecution, and providing that no religious test shall ever be required.

A Landholder[22]

William Williams, *February 11, 1788*

When the clause in the 6th article,[23] which provides that "no religious test should ever be required as a qualification to any office

---

22. The pseudonym under which Oliver Ellsworth wrote.
23. Of the U.S. Constitution.

or trust, etc." came under consideration[,] I observed I should have chose that sentence and any thing relating to a religious test, had been totally omitted rather than stand as it did, but still more wished something of the kind should have been inserted, but with a reverse sense, so far as to require an explicit acknowledgment of the being of a God, his perfections and his providence, and to have been prefixed to, and stand as, the first introductory words of the Constitution, in the following or similar terms, viz.[24] *We the people of the United States, in a firm belief of the being and perfections of the one living and true God, the creator and supreme Governour of the world, in his universal providence and the authority of his laws: that he will require of all moral agents an account of their conduct, that all rightful powers among men are ordained of, and mediately derived from God, therefore in a dependence on his blessing and acknowledgment of his efficient protection in establishing our Independence, whereby it is become necessary to agree upon and settle a Constitution of federal government for ourselves,* and in order to form a more perfect union etc. as it is expressed in the present introduction, do ordain etc. And instead of none, that no other religious test should ever be required etc. And that supposing, but not granting, this would *be no security at all,* that it would make hypocrites etc. Yet this would not be a sufficient reason against it; as it would be a public declaration against, and disapprobation of men, who did not, even with sincerity, make such a profession, and they must be left to the searcher of hearts; that it would however, be the voice of the great body of the people, and an acknowledgment proper and highly becoming them to express on this great and only occasion, and according to the course of Providence, one mean[s] of

24. That is.

obtaining blessings from the most high. But that since it was not, and so difficult and dubious to get it inserted, I would not wish to make it a capital objection; that I had no more idea of a religious test, which should restrain offices to any particular sect, class, or denomination of men or christians, in the long list of diversity, than to regulate their bestowments, by the stature or dress of the candidate; nor did I believe one sensible catholic man in the state wished for such a limitation; and that therefore the News-Paper observations, and reasonings (I named no author) against a test, in favour of any one denomination of christians, and the sacrilegious injunctions of the test laws of England etc. combated objections which did not exist, and *was building up a man of straw and knocking him down again.* These are the same and only ideas and sentiments, I endeavored to communicate on that subject, tho' perhaps not precisely in the same terms; as I had not written, nor preconceived them, except the proposed test, and whether there is any reason in them or not, I submit to the public.

I freely confess such a test and acknowledgment, would have given me great additional satisfaction: and I conceive the arguments against it, on the score of hypocrisy, would apply with equal force against requiring an oath, from any officer of the united or individual states; and with little abatement, to any oath in any case whatever: but divine and human wisdom, with universal experience, have approved and established them as useful, and a security to mankind.

I thought it was my duty to make the observations, in this behalf, which I did, and to bear my testimony for God: and that it was also my duty to say *the Constitution,* with this, and some other faults of another kind, was yet too wise and too necessary to be rejected.

W. Williams

P.S. I could not have suspected, the Landholder (if I know him) to be the author of the piece referred to; but if he or any other, is pleased to reply, without the signature of his proper name, he will receive no further answer or notice from me.

6. BENJAMIN RUSH WISHES GOD WAS MENTIONED IN THE CONSTITUTION, 1789

Benjamin Rush, a Philadelphia physician and signer of the Declaration of Independence, regretted that the Constitution did not mention God. In a letter to Vice President John Adams in 1789, he complained that "many pious people wish the name of the Supreme Being had been introduced somewhere in the new Constitution." Although Rush supported the ratification of the Constitution, his views were similar to some Anti-Federalists, who also wished that God's name had been mentioned somewhere in the document.

> From Benjamin Rush to John Adams, June 15, 1789, in *Adams Papers, 1639–1889*, microfilm edition, 608 reels (Boston, Massachusetts Historical Society, 1954–1959), reel 372. Used by permission of the Massachusetts Historical Society.
>
> Dear Sir, Philadelphia, June 15th, 1789 . . .
>
>  Many pious people wish the name of the Supreme Being had been introduced somewhere in the new Constitution. Perhaps an acknowledgement may be made of his goodness or of his providence in the proposed amendments. In all enterprises and parties I believe the *praying* are better allies than the *fighting* part of communities.
>
> I am, dear sir, with great regard, your affectionate and steady friend,
>
> BENJN RUSH

7. DEBATES ON THE RELIGION CLAUSES OF THE FIRST AMENDMENT, 1789

James Madison had to promise reluctant supporters of the new Constitution that he would secure amendments to the Constitution in the first Congress, after the Constitution was ratified. Religious freedom was one of the most fundamental rights that many Americans felt the Constitution needed to ensure. In this document, we see part of Madison and Congress's work in framing the religion clauses of the First Amendment, which was ultimately ratified by the states in 1791.

From *The Debates and Proceedings in the Congress of the United States,* March 3, 1789–March 3, 1791 (Washington, DC, 1834), 1:757–759.

Saturday, August 15.

AMENDMENTS TO THE CONSTITUTION.

The House again went into a Committee of the whole on the proposed amendments to the constitution, Mr. Boudinot[25] in the chair.

The fourth proposition being under consideration, as follows:

Article 1.Section 9. Between paragraphs two and three insert "no religion shall be established by law, nor shall the equal rights of conscience be infringed."

Mr. Sylvester[26] had some doubts of the propriety of the mode of expression used in this paragraph. He apprehended that it was liable to a construction different from what had been made by

25. Elias Boudinot, representative from New Jersey.
26. Peter Sylvester (or Silvester), representative from New York.

the committee. He feared it might be thought to have a tendency to abolish religion altogether.

Mr. Vining[27] suggested the propriety of transposing the two members of the sentence.

Mr. Gerry[28] said it would read better if it was, that no religious doctrine shall be established by law.

Mr. Sherman[29] thought the amendment altogether unnecessary, inasmuch as Congress had no authority whatever delegated to them by the constitution to make religious establishments; he would, therefore, move to have it struck out.

Mr. Carroll[30],—As the rights of conscience are, in their nature, of peculiar delicacy, and will little bear the gentlest touch of governmental hand; and as many sects have concurred in opinion that they are not well secured under the present constitution, he said he was much in favor of adopting the words. He thought it would tend more towards conciliating the minds of the people to the Government than almost any other amendment he had heard proposed. He would not contend with gentlemen about the phraseology, his object was to secure the substance in such a manner as to satisfy the wishes of the honest part of the community.

Mr. Madison said, he apprehended the meaning of the words to be, that Congress should not establish a religion, and enforce the legal observation of it by law, nor compel men to worship God in any manner contrary to their conscience. Whether the words are necessary or not, he did not mean to say, but they had

27. John Vining, representative from Delaware.
28. Elbridge Gerry, representative from Massachusetts and future vice president of the United States under James Madison.
29. Roger Sherman, representative from Connecticut, who signed both the Declaration of Independence and the U.S. Constitution.
30. Daniel Carroll, representative from Maryland, who also signed the Constitution.

been required by some of the State Conventions, who seemed to entertain an opinion that under the clause of the constitution, which gave power to Congress to make all laws necessary and proper to carry into execution the constitution, and the laws made under it, enabled them to make laws of such a nature as might infringe the rights of conscience, and establish a national religion; to prevent these effects he presumed the amendment was intended, and he thought it as well expressed as the nature of the language would admit.

Mr. Huntington[31] said that he feared, with the gentleman first up on this subject, that the words might be taken in such latitude as to be extremely hurtful to the cause of religion. He understood the amendment to mean what had been expressed by the gentleman from Virginia; but others might find it convenient to put another construction upon it. The ministers of their congregations to the Eastward were maintained by the contributions of those who belonged to their society; the expense of building meeting-houses was contributed in the same manner. These things were regulated by by-laws. If an action was brought before a Federal Court on any of these cases, the person who had neglected to perform his engagements could not be compelled to do it; for a support of ministers, or building of places of worship might be construed into a religious establishment.

By the charter of Rhode Island, no religion could be established by law; he could give a history of the effects of such a regulation; indeed the people were now enjoying the blessed fruits of it. He hoped, therefore, the amendment would be made in such a way as to secure the rights of conscience, and a free

---

31. Benjamin Huntington, representative from Connecticut, who had served as a general in the Revolutionary War.

exercise of the rights of religion, but not to patronize those who professed no religion at all.

Mr. Madison thought, if the word national was inserted before religion, it would satisfy the minds of honorable gentlemen. He believed that the people feared one sect might obtain a pre-eminence, or two combine together, and establish a religion to which they would compel others to conform. He thought if the word national was introduced, it would point the amendment directly to the object it was intended to prevent.

Mr. Livermore[32] was not satisfied with that amendment; but he did not wish them to dwell long on the subject. He thought it would be better if it was altered, and made to read in this manner, that Congress shall make no laws touching religion, or infringing the rights of conscience.

Mr. Gerry did not like the term national, proposed by the gentleman from Virginia, and he hoped it would not be adopted by the House. It brought to his mind some observations that had taken place in the conventions at the time they were considering the present constitution. It had been insisted upon by those who were called antifederalists, that this form of Government consolidated the Union; the honorable gentleman's motion shows that he considers it in the same light. Those who were called antifederalists at that time complained that they had injustice done them by the title, because they were in favor of a Federal Government, and the others were in favor of a national one; the federalists were for ratifying the constitution as it stood, and the others not until amendments were made. Their names then ought not to have been distinguished by federalists and antifederalists, but rats and antirats.

32. Samuel Livermore, representative from New Hampshire.

Mr. Madison withdrew his motion, but observed that the words "no national religion shall be established by law," did not imply that the Government was a national one . . .

8. FIRST AMENDMENT OF THE U.S. CONSTITUTION, 1791

The religion clauses of the First Amendment—the establishment clause and the free exercise clause—were means of protecting religious liberty in the new republic. Although members of Congress could not reach a consensus about what religious liberty meant, at the very least it was agreed that the federal government should not interfere with the "free exercise" of religion or support a state-sponsored church.

> First Amendment, U.S. Constitution, 1791, in Richard Peters, ed., *The Public Statutes at Large of the United States of America* (Boston, 1845), 1:21.
>
> Congress[33] shall make no law respecting an establishment of religion, or prohibiting the free exercise thereof; or abridging the freedom of speech, or of the press; or the right of the people peaceably to assemble, and to petition the government for a redress of grievances.

9. MINISTERS LAMENT THE "GODLESS" CONSTITUTION, 1812, 1815

In 1812 Americans were engulfed in another war with England. Many ministers believed that Americans' rampant materialism and blatant disregard for religion provoked the wrath of the Almighty upon

33. The U.S. Congress.

them. Decrying the affairs of the nation, Protestant pastors harked back to the Constitution, blaming this "godless" state on the Founding Fathers who forgot God in forming their framework of government. Timothy Dwight, president of Yale College and a prominent Congregationalist minister, delivered this sermon at New Haven, Connecticut, on July 23, 1812, denouncing the framers for writing a Constitution "without any acknowledgement of God." A second minister, Alexander McLeod, one of the editors of the *Christian Magazine* and a prominent Presbyterian from New York City, delivered a second rebuke in 1815. He faulted the Founders for both the absence of God in the Constitution and their acceptance of slavery.

From Timothy Dwight, *A Discourse in Two Parts, Delivered on July 23, 1812, on the PUBLIC FAST, in The Chapel of Yale College,* 2nd ed. (Boston, 1813), 24; Alexander McLeod, *A Scriptural View of the Character, Causes and Ends of the Present War,* 2nd ed. (New York, 1815), 53–55.

Timothy Dwight *sermon on July 23, 1812:*

Notwithstanding the prevalence of religion, which I have described, the irreligion and the wickedness of our land are such, as to furnish a most painful and melancholy prospect to a serious mind. We formed our Constitution without any acknowledgement of God; without any recognition of his mercies to us, as a people, of his government, or even of his existence. The Convention, by which it was formed, never asked, even once, his direction, or his blessing upon their labours. Thus we commenced our national existence under the present system, without God. I wish I could say, that a disposition to render him the reverence, *due to his* great *name,* and the gratitude, demanded by his innumerable mercies, had been more public, visible, uniform, and fervent.

Alexander McLeod *sermon in 1815:*

The sin of a nation is the aggregate of all the transgressions committed by individuals in that nation: but these are properly *national sins*, which are notorious, prevalent, and characteristic. I speak not, however, of the nation at large, but of its constituted authorities, and therefore attend only AUTHORIZED SINS.

The public immoralities of the constitution of our federal government, may, although more numerous in detail, be classed under two heads, viz. *Disrespect for God—and violation of human liberty.* By the terms of the national compact,[34] God is not at all acknowledged, and holding men in slavery is authorized. Both these are evils.

... In a federative[35] government, erected over several distinct and independent states, retaining each the power of local legislation, it is not to be expected that specific provision should be made for the interests of religion in particular congregations. The general government is erected for the general good of the United States, and especially for the management of their foreign concerns: but no association of men for moral purposes can be justified in an entire neglect of the Sovereign of the world. Statesmen in this country had undoubtedly in their eye the abuse of religion for mere political purposes, which in the nations of the old world, had corrupted the sanctuary, and laid the foundation for the persecution of godly men ... But no consideration will justify

34. U.S. Constitution.
35. An eighteenth-century term connoting a league of sovereign states.

the framers of the federal constitution, and the administration of the government, in withholding a recognition of *the Lord and his Anointed* from the grand charter of the nation. On our daily bread, we ask a blessing. At our ordinary meals, we acknowledge the Lord of the world. We begin our last testament for disposing of worldly estates, in the name of God: and shall we be guiltless, with the bible in our hands, to disclaim the Christian religion as a body politic?

10. JAMES MADISON'S "DETACHED MEMORANDA," CIRCA 1817–1832

Sometime after his retirement from the presidency in 1817, James Madison wrote the "Detached Memoranda," which gave him an opportunity to reflect on his political career. In this excerpt, Madison expressed his concern that the American government had too often violated the proper boundary between church and state, even in the appointment of chaplains and the observation of days of prayer and fasting. Madison always embraced a robust separation of church and state, and in his retirement those views seemed to grow even stronger.

> From Elizabeth Fleet, ed., "Madison's 'Detached Memoranda,'" *William and Mary Quarterly*, 3d ser., 3, no. 4 (October 1946): 554–562. Used by permission of the Omohundro Institute of Early American History and Culture at the College of William and Mary.

> The danger of silent accumulations & encroachments by Ecclesiastical Bodies have not sufficiently engaged attention in the U.S. They have the noble merit of first unshackling the

conscience from persecuting laws, and of establishing among religious Sects a legal equality. If some of the States have not embraced this just and this truly Xn[36] principle in its proper latitude, all of them present examples by which the most enlightened States of the old world may be instructed; and there is one State at least, Virginia, where religious liberty is placed on its true foundation and is defined in its full latitude. The general principle is contained in her declaration of rights, prefixed to her Constitution: but it is unfolded and defined, in its precise extent, in the act of the Legislature, usually named the Religious Bill, which passed into a law in the year 1786. Here the separation between the authority of human laws, and the natural rights of Man excepted from the grant on which all political authority is founded, is traced as distinctly as words can admit, and the limits to this authority established with as much solemnity as the forms of legislation can express. The law has the further advantage of having been the result of a formal appeal to the sense of the Community and a deliberate sanction of a vast majority, comprizing every sect of Christians in the State. This act is a true standard of Religious liberty: its principle the great barrier agst[37] usurpations on the rights of conscience. As long as it is respected & no longer, these will be safe. Every provision for them short of this principle, will be found to leave crevices at least thro' which bigotry may introduce persecution; a monster, that feeding & thriving on its own venom, gradually swells to a size and strength overwhelming all laws divine & human.

Ye States of America, which retain in your Constitutions or Codes, any aberration from the sacred principle of religious

36. Christian.
37. Against.

liberty, by giving to Caesar what belongs to God, or joining together what God has put asunder, hasten to revise & purify your systems, and make the example of your Country as pure & compleat, in what relates to the freedom of the mind and its allegiance to its maker, as in what belongs to the legitimate objects of political & civil institutions.

Strongly guarded as is the separation between Religion & Govt in the Constitution of the United States the danger of encroachment by Ecclesiastical Bodies, may be illustrated by precedents already furnished in their short history. (See the cases in which negatives were put by J.M. on two bills passd by Congs and his signature withheld from another. See also attempt in Kentucky for example, where it was proposed to exempt Houses of Worship from taxes.[ )][38]

The most notable attempt was that in Virga to establish a Genl assessment for the support of all Xn sects. This was proposed in the year [1784] by P.H.[39] and supported by all his eloquence, aided by the remaining prejudices of the Sect which before the Revolution had been established by law. The progress of the measure was arrested by urging that the respect due to the people required in so extraordinary a case an appeal to their deliberate will. The bill was accordingly printed & published with that view. At the instance of Col: George Nicholas, Col: George Mason & others, the memorial & remonstrance agst it was drawn up, (which see) and printed Copies of it circulated thro' the State, to be signed by the people at large. It met with the approbation of the Baptists, the Presbyterians, the Quakers, and

---

38. As president, Madison had vetoed bills that would have incorporated the Episcopal church in Alexandria, Virginia, and reserved land for a Baptist church in Mississippi.

39. Patrick Henry.

the few Roman Catholics, universally; of the Methodists in part; and even of not a few of the Sect formerly established by the law.[40] When the Legislature assembled, the number of Copies & signatures prescribed displayed such an overwhelming opposition of the people, that the proposed plan of a genl assessmt was crushed under it; and advantage taken of the crisis to carry thro' the Legisl: the Bill above referred to, establishing religious liberty. In the course of the opposition to the bill in the House of Delegates, which was warm & strenuous from some of the minority, an experiment was made on the reverence entertained for the name & sanctity of the Saviour, by proposing to insert the words "Jesus Christ" after the words "our lord" in the preamble, the object of which, would have been, to imply a restriction of the liberty defined in the Bill, to those professing his religion only. The amendment was discussed, and rejected . . . The opponents of the amendment having turned the feeling as well as judgment of the House agst it, by successfully contending that the better proof of reverence for that holy name wd[41] be not to profane it by making it a topic of legisl. discussion, & particularly by making his religion the means of abridging the natural and equal rights of all men, in defiance of his own declaration that his Kingdom was not of this world. This view of the subject was much enforced by the circumstance that it was espoused by some members who were particularly distinguished by their reputed piety and Christian zeal . . .

Is the appointment of Chaplains to the two Houses of Congress consistent with the Constitution, and with the pure principle of religious freedom?

In strictness the answer on both points must be in the negative. The Constitution of the U.S. forbids everything like an establishment of a national religion. The law appointing Chaplains establishes a religious worship for the national representatives, to be performed by Ministers of religion, elected by a majority of them; and these are to be paid out of the national taxes. Does not this involve the principle of a national establishment, applicable to a provision for a religious worship for the Constituent as well as of the representative Body, approved by the majority, and conducted by Ministers of religion paid by the entire nation.

The establishment of the chaplainship to Congs is a palpable violation of equal rights, as well as of Constitutional principles: The tenets of the chaplains elected [by the majority] shut the door of worship agst the members whose creeds & consciences forbid a participation in that of the majority. To say nothing of other sects, this is the case with that of Roman Catholics & Quakers who have always had members in one or both of the Legislative branches. Could a Catholic clergyman ever hope to be appointed a Chaplain? To say that his religious principles are obnoxious or that his sect is small, is to lift the evil at once and exhibit in its naked deformity the doctrine that religious truth is to be tested by numbers, or that the major sects have a right to govern the minor.

If Religion consist in voluntary acts of individuals, singly, or voluntarily associated, and it be proper that public functionaries, as well as their Constituents sh[oul]d discharge their religious duties, let them like their Constituents, do so at their own expence. How small a contribution from each member of Congs wd suffice for the purpose? How just wd it be in its principle? How noble in its exemplary sacrifice to the genius of the

Constitution; and the divine right of conscience? Why should the expence of a religious worship be allowed for the Legislature, be paid by the public, more than that for the Ex[ecutive] or Judiciary branch of the Govt

Were the establishment to be tried by its fruits, are not the daily devotions conducted by these legal Ecclesiastics, already degenerating into a scanty attendance, and a tiresome formality?

Rather than let this step beyond the landmarks of power have the effect of a legitimate precedent, it will be better to apply to it the legal aphorism de minimis non curat lex: or to class it cum "maculis quas aut incuria fudit, aut humana parum cavit natura."[42]

Better also to disarm in the same way, the precedent of Chaplainships for the army and navy, than erect them into a political authority in matters of religion. The object of this establishment is seducing; the motive to it is laudable. But is it not safer to adhere to a right principle, and trust to its consequences, than confide in the reasoning however specious in favor of a wrong one. Look thro' the armies & navies of the world, and say whether in the appointment of their ministers of religion, the spiritual interest of the flocks or the temporal interest of the Shepherds, be most in view: whether here, as elsewhere the political care of religion is not a nominal more than a real aid. If the spirit of armies be devout, the spirit out of the armies will never be less so; and a failure of religious instruction & exhortation from a voluntary source within or without, will rarely happen: and if such be not the spirit of armies, the official services of their Teachers are not likely to produce it. It

---

42. Quoting from the Roman philosopher Horace, this sentence means, "The law does not have concern for little things: or to class it with 'blemishes which either carelessness pours forth, or human nature too little takes guard against.'"

is more likely to flow from the labours of a spontaneous zeal. The armies of the Puritans had their appointed Chaplains; but without these there would have been no lack of public devotion in that devout age.

The case of navies with insulated crews may be less within the scope of these reflections. But it is not entirely so. The chance of a devout officer, might be of as much worth to religion, as the service of an ordinary chaplain. [were it admitted that religion has a real interest in the latter.] But we are always to keep in mind that it is safer to trust the consequences of a right principle, than reasonings in support of a bad one.

Religious proclamations by the Executive recommending thanksgivings & fasts are shoots from the same root with the legislative acts reviewed.

Altho' recommendations only, they imply a religious agency, making no part of the trust delegated to political rulers.

The objections to them are 1. that Govts ought not to interpose in relation to those subject to their authority but in cases where they can do it with effect. And *advisory* Govt is a contradiction in terms. 2. The members of a Govt as such can in no sense, be regarded as possessing an advisory trust from their Constituents in their religious capacities. They cannot form an ecclesiastical Assembly, Convocation, Council, or Synod, and as such issue decrees or injunctions addressed to the faith or the Consciences of the people. In their individual capacities, as distinct from their official station, they might unite in recommendations of any sort whatever, in the same manner as any other individuals might do. But then their recommendations ought to express the true character from which they emanate. 3. They seem to imply and certainly nourish the erronious idea of a *national* religion. The idea just as it related to the Jewish nation under a theocracy, having been improperly adopted by so many nations which having been embraced Xnity, is too apt to lurk in the bosoms even of Americans, who in general are aware of the distinction between religious & political societies. The idea also of a union of all to form one nation under one Govt in acts of devotion to the God of all is an imposing idea. But reason and the principles of the Xn religion require that all the individuals composing a nation even of the same precise creed & wished to unite in a universal act of religion at the same time, the union ought to be effected thro' the intervention of their religious not of their political representatives. In a nation composed of various sects, some alienated widely from others, and where no agreement could take place thro' the former, the interposition of the latter is doubly wrong: 4. The tendency of the practice, to narrow the recommendation to the standard of the predominant sect. The 1st proclamation of Genl Washington dated January 1, 1795 (see if this was the 1st)[43] recommending a day of thanksgiving, embraced all who believed in a supreme ruler of the Universe. That of Mr Adams called for a *Xn* worship. Many private letters reproached the Proclamations issued by J.M. for using general terms, used in that of President W—n; and some of them for not inserting particulars according with the faith of certain Xn sects. The practice if not strictly guarded naturally terminates in a conformity to the creed of the majority and a single sect, if amounting to a majority. 5. The last & not the least objection is the liability of the practice to a subserviency to political views; to the scandal of religion, as well as the increase of party animosities. Candid or incautious politicians will not always disown

---

43. Washington issued his first Thanksgiving proclamation on October 3, 1789, to be observed on Thursday, November 26.

such views. In truth it is difficult to frame such a religious Proclamation generally suggested by a political State of things, without referring to them in terms having some bearing on party questions. The Proclamation of Pres: W. which was issued just after the suppression of the Insurrection in Penna[44] and at a time when the public mind was divided on several topics, was so construed by many. Of this the Secretary of State himself, E. Randolph seems to have had an anticipation.

The original draught of that Instrument filed in the Dept. of State (see copies of these papers on the files of J.M.) in the hand writing of Mr Hamilton the Secretary of the Treasury. It appears that several slight alterations only had been made at the suggestion of the Secretary of State; and in a marginal note in his hand, it is remarked that "In short this proclamation ought to savour as much as possible of religion, & not too much of having a political object." In a subjoined note in the hand of Mr. Hamilton, this remark is answered by the counter-remark that "A proclamation of a Government which is a national act, naturally embraces objects which are political" so *naturally*, is the idea of policy associated with religion, whatever be the mode or the occasion, when a function of the latter is assumed by those in power.

During the administration of Mr Jefferson no religious proclamation was issued. It being understood that his successor was disinclined to such interpositions of the Executive and by some supposed moreover that they might originate with more propriety with the Legislative Body, a resolution was passed requesting him to issue a proclamation. (see the resolution in the Journals of Congress.[)]

44. The Whiskey Rebellion of 1794.

It was thought not proper to refuse a compliance altogether; but a form & language were employed, which were meant to deaden as much as possible any claim of political right to enjoin religious observances by resting these expressly on the voluntary compliance of individuals, and even by limiting the recommendation to such as wished simultaneous as well as voluntary performance of a religious act on the occasion.

Chapter 4

Religion and the Federal Government

1. CONGRESSIONAL CHAPLAINS, 1789

During the American Revolution the Continental Congress often opened its proceedings with prayer, which was led by a clergyman who was paid by the Congress. In keeping with this tradition, the First Congress passed a measure in 1789 authorizing the appointment of and pay for congressional chaplains. Although Thomas Jefferson and later James Madison opposed the practice, the measure passed, setting a precedent for a chaplaincy system that is still in effect today.

> From Congressional Chaplains Act, reprinted in *The Debates and Proceedings in the Congress of the United States* (Washington, DC, 1834), 1:19, 24, 242; "An Act for Compensation . . .," reprinted in *The Public Statutes at Large of the United States of America*, ed. Richard Peters (Boston, 1845), 1:71.

Wednesday, April 15, 1789

The committee appointed the 7th of April, to prepare a system of rules to govern the two Houses in cases of conference, to take into consideration the manner of electing chaplains, and to confer thereon with a committee of the House of Representatives, reported:

That they had conferred with a committee of the House of Representatives, for that purpose appointed. . . .

The committee abovementioned further reported.

That two chaplains, of different denominations, be appointed to Congress for the present session, the Senate to appoint one, and give notice thereof to the House of Representatives, who shall, thereupon, appoint the other; which chaplains shall commence their services in the Houses that appoint them, but shall interchange weekly.

Which was also accepted.

Saturday, April 25, 1789

The Right Reverend Samuel Provost[1] was elected Chaplain [of the Senate].

Friday, May 1, 1789

The House then proceeded by ballot to the appointment of a Chaplain to Congress on the part of this House. Upon examining the ballots, it appeared that the Rev. William Linn[2] was elected.

September 22, 1789

Chap. XVII.—An Act for allowing Compensation to the Members of the Senate and House of Representatives of the United States, and to the Officers of both Houses.

1. Samuel Provost was an Episcopal bishop of New York.
2. William Linn was a Dutch Reformed clergyman of New York City and one of the first chaplains in the U.S. Congress.

Sec. 4. *And be it further enacted,* That there shall be allowed to each chaplain of Congress, at the rate of five hundred dollars per annum during the session of Congress; to the secretary of the Senate and clerk of the House of Representatives, fifteen hundred dollars per annum each, to commence from the time of their respective appointments; and also a further allowance of two dollars per day to each, during the session of that branch for which he officiates. . . .

2. GEORGE WASHINGTON'S THANKSGIVING PROCLAMATION, 1789

During the Revolutionary War, the Continental Congress frequently called for national days of prayer and thanksgiving. This appeal to religious authority was designed to invoke God's blessings on the Congress, the Continental Army, and Americans in time of crisis. George Washington continued this practice during his first term in office—a practice that was suspended by Thomas Jefferson, reinstated by James Madison, then continued by other presidents to the present day. In this Thanksgiving proclamation, the nation's first under the new Constitution, Washington asked Americans to acknowledge God's hand in helping them achieve victory against the British during the Revolutionary War. He also implored them to recognize God's presence in forming the new government. The Thanksgiving Proclamation, as it became known, was published in many American newspapers across the country.

From John C. Fitzpatrick, ed., *The Writings of George Washington, from the Original Manuscript Sources, 1745–1799,* 39 vols. (Washington, DC, 1931–1944), 30:427–428.

Whereas it is the duty of all Nations to acknowledge the providence of Almighty God, to obey his will, to be grateful for his benefits, and humbly to implore his protection and favor, and Whereas both Houses of Congress have by their joint Committee requested me "to recommend to the People of the United States a day of public thanks-giving and prayer to be observed by acknowledging with grateful hearts the many signal favors of Almighty God, especially by affording them an opportunity peaceably to establish a form of government for their safety and happiness."

Now therefore I do recommend and assign Thursday the 26th. day of November next to be devoted by the People of these States to the service of that great and glorious Being, who is the beneficent Author of all the good that was, that is, or that will be. That we may then all unite in rendering unto him our sincere and humble thanks, for his kind care and protection of the People of this country previous to their becoming a Nation, for the signal and manifold mercies, and the favorable interpositions of his providence, which we experienced in the course and conclusion of the late war, for the great degree of tranquillity, union, and plenty, which we have since enjoyed, for the peaceable and rational manner in which we have been enabled to establish constitutions of government for our safety and happiness, and particularly the national One now lately instituted, for the civil and religious liberty with which we are blessed, and the means we have of acquiring and diffusing useful knowledge and in general for all the great and various favors which he hath been pleased to confer upon us.

And also that we may then unite in most humbly offering our prayers and supplications to the great Lord and Ruler of Nations and beseech him to pardon our national and other transgressions, to enable us all, whether in public or private stations, to perform our several and relative duties properly and punctually, to render our national government a blessing to all the People, by constantly being a government of wise, just and constitutional laws, discreetly and faithfully executed and obeyed, to protect and guide all Sovereigns and Nations (especially such as have shown kindness unto us) and to bless them with good government, peace, and concord. To promote the knowledge and practice of true religion and virtue, and the encrease of science among them and Us, and generally to grant unto all Mankind such a degree of temporal prosperity as he alone knows to be best.

3. GEORGE WASHINGTON'S FAREWELL ADDRESS, 1796

One of the most famous speeches in American history is George Washington's Farewell Address, delivered in 1796, at the close of his second term. By then, Washington had become exasperated with partisan politics. In the mid-1790s, political factions had formed, pitting his secretary of treasury, Alexander Hamilton, against his secretary of state, Thomas Jefferson. They had competing visions about how the country should be run. Hamilton wanted a bold, energetic national government run by the rich and wellborn—a nation dominated by elite merchants and profit-driven manufacturers. Jefferson envisioned a small government that would be local and close to the people—a nation dominated by independent farmers. Washington's Farewell Address addresses these competing visions. It reflects his concern about harmony and unity in politics, and the need for the civil government to be rooted in a strong moral and religious foundation.

From *Washington's Farewell Address, the Proclamation of Jackson against Nullification, and the Declaration of Independence* (Washington, DC, 1862), 4–5, 8–9, 11.

In looking forward to the moment which is intended to terminate the career of my public life, my feelings do not permit me to suspend the deep acknowledgment of that debt of gratitude which I owe to my beloved country for the many honors it has conferred upon me; still more for the steadfast confidence with which it has supported me; and for the opportunities I have thence enjoyed of manifesting my inviolable attachment, by services faithful and persevering, though in usefulness unequal to my zeal. If benefits have resulted to our country from these services, let it always be remembered to your praise, and as an instructive example in our annals, that, under circumstances in which the passions, agitated in every direction, were liable to mislead, amidst appearances sometimes dubious, vicissitudes of fortune, often discouraging in situations in which, not unfrequently, want of success has countenanced the spirit of criticism, the constancy of your support was the essential prop of the efforts, and a guarantee of the plans by which they were effected. Profoundly penetrated with this idea, I shall carry it with me to my grave, as a strong incitement to unceasing vows, that heaven may continue to you the choicest tokens of its beneficence; that your union and brotherly affection may be perpetual; that the free Constitution, which is the work of your hands, may be sacredly maintained; that its administration, in every department, may be stamped with wisdom and virtue; that, in fine, the happiness of the people of these States, under the auspices of liberty, may be made complete, by so careful a preservation, and so prudent a use of this blessing, as will acquire to them the glory of recommending it to the applause, the affection, and adoption of every nation which is yet a stranger to it.

Here, perhaps, I ought to stop; but a solicitude for your welfare, which cannot end but with my life, and the apprehension of danger natural to that solicitude, urge me, on an occasion like the present, to offer to your solemn contemplation, and to recommend to your frequent review, some sentiments, which are the result of much reflection—of no inconsiderable observation—and which appear to me all important to the permanency of your felicity as a people. These will be offered to you with the more freedom, as you can only see in them the disinterested warnings of a parting friend, who can possibly have no personal motive to bias his counsel; nor can I forget, as an encouragement to it, your indulgent reception of my sentiments on a former and not dissimilar occasion.

Interwoven as is the love of liberty with every ligament of your hearts, no recommendation of mine is necessary to fortify or confirm the attachment.

The unity of government, which constitutes you one people, is also now dear to you. It is justly so, for it is a main pillar in the edifice of your real independence; the support of your tranquility at home, your peace abroad; of your safety; of your prosperity; of that very liberty which you so highly prize. But as it is easy to foresee that, from different causes and from different quarters, much pains will be taken, many artifices employed, to weaken in your minds the conviction of this truth—as this is the point in your political fortress against which the batteries of internal and external enemies will be most constantly and actively (though often covertly and insidiously) directed—it is of infinite moment that you should properly estimate the immense value of your national Union to your collective and individual happiness; that you should cherish a cordial, habitual, and immovable attachment to it; accustoming yourselves to think and speak of it as of the palladium of your political safety and prosperity; watching for its preservation with jealous anxiety; discountenancing whatever may suggest even a suspicion that it can, in any event, be abandoned; and indignantly frowning upon the first dawning of every attempt to alienate any portion of our country from the rest, or to enfeeble the sacred ties which now link together the various parts. . . .

Of all the dispositions and habits which lead to political prosperity, religion and morality are indispensable supports. In vain would that man claim the tribute of patriotism, who should labor to subvert these great pillars of human happiness, these firmest props of the duties of men and citizens. The mere politician, equally with the pious man, ought to respect and cherish them. A volume could not trace all their connexions with private and public felicity. Let it simply be asked; where is the security for property, for reputation, for life, if the sense of religious obligation desert the oaths, which are the instruments of investigation in courts of justice? And let us with caution indulge the supposition that morality can be maintained without religion. Whatever may be conceded to the influence of refined education on minds of peculiar structure, reason and experience both forbid us to expect that national morality can prevail in exclusion of religious principle.

It is substantially true that virtue or morality is a necessary spring of popular government. The rule indeed extends, with more or less force, to every species of free government. Who, that is a sincere friend to it, can look with indifference upon attempts to shake the foundation of the fabric?

Promote then, as an object of primary importance, institutions for the general diffusion of knowledge. In proportion as the structure of a government gives force to public opinion, it is essential that public opinion should be enlightened. . . .

Observe good faith and justice towards all nations; cultivate peace and harmony with all. Religion and morality enjoin this conduct; and can it be that good policy does not equally enjoy it?—It will be worthy of a free, enlightened, and, at no distant period, a great nation, to give to mankind the magnanimous and too novel example of a people always guided by an exalted justice and benevolence. Who can doubt but, in the course of time and things, the fruits of such a plan would richly repay any temporary advantages which might be lost by a steady adherence to it? Can it be that Providence has not connected the permanent felicity of a nation with its virtue? The experiment, at least, is recommended by every sentiment which ennobles human nature. Alas! is it rendered impossible by its vices? . . .

In offering to you, my countrymen, these counsels of an old and affectionate friend, I dare not hope they will make the strong and lasting impression I could wish; that they will control the usual current of the passions, or prevent our nation from running the course which has hitherto marked the destiny of nations; but if I may even flatter myself that they may be productive of some partial benefit, some occasional good; that they may now and then recur to moderate the fury of party spirit, to warn against the mischiefs of foreign intrigues, to guard against the impostures of pretended patriotism, this hope will be a full recompense for the solicitude for your welfare by which they have been dictated.

4. TREATY OF TRIPOLI, 1797

Near the end of President George Washington's second term in 1796, Joel Barlow of Connecticut, a diplomat and known Deist, penned a carefully worded treaty that was designed to end attacks by Barbary pirates on American ships. Barlow inserted a phrase in the treaty stating that the American government was not founded on the Christian religion. The treaty was submitted for formal debate in 1797 during John Adams's administration, and it was signed by him and ratified by two-thirds of the U.S. Senate that same year. Although there is no equivalent phrase in the Arabic version of the treaty, contemporary newspapers published it in the full text, which led some critics to complain that Barlow was "trampling upon the cross" of Christ. In 1805, when diplomat Tobias Lear negotiated a new treaty for the Jefferson administration, the phrase was dropped.

From *Naval Documents Related to the United States Wars with the Barbary Powers*, 6 vols. (Washington, DC, 1939–1944), 1:177–179.

Annals of Congress, 5th Congress

Article 1. There is a firm and perpetual peace and friendship between the United States of America and the Bey and subjects of Tripoli, of Barbary, made by the free consent of both parties, and guarantied by the most potent Dey and Regency of Algiers....

Art. 11. As the Government of the United States of America is not, in any sense, founded on the Christian religion; as it has in itself no character of enmity against the laws, religion, or tranquillity, of Mussulmen;[3] and, as the said States never entered into any war, or act of hostility against any Mahometan nation,[4] it is declared by the parties, that no pretext arising from religious opinions, shall ever produce an interruption of the harmony existing between the two countries.

3. Muslims or followers of Islam.
4. An Islamic country.

Art. 12. In case of any dispute, arising from a violation of any of the articles of this treaty, no appeal shall be made to arms; nor shall war be declared on any pretext whatever. But if the Consul, residing at the place where the dispute shall happen, shall not be able to settle the same, an amicable referrence shall be made to the mutual friend of the parties, the Dey of Algiers; the parties hereby engaging to abide by his decision. And he, by virtue of his signature to this treaty, engages for himself and successors to declare the justice of the case, according to the true interpretation of the treaty, and to use all the means in his power to enforce the observance of the same.

Signed and sealed at Tripoli of Barbary the 3d day of Junad in the year of the Hegira[5] 1211—corresponding with the 4th day of November, 1796, by

JUSSOF BASHAW MAHOMET, *Bey.*

MAMET, *Treasurer.*

AMET, *Minister of Marine.*

SOLIMAN KAYA.

GALIL, *General of the Troops.*

MAHOMET, *Commander of the City.*

AMET, *Chamberlain.*

ALLY, *Chief of the Divan.*

MAMET, *Secretary.*

Signed and sealed at Algiers, the 4th day of Argill, 1211—corresponding with the 3d day of January, 1797, by

HASSAN BASHAW, *Dey,*

And by the agent Plenipotentiary of the United States of America,

JOEL BARLOW.

---

5. Refers to the flight of Muhammad from Mecca to Medina in 622 AD.

5. JOHN ADAMS PROCLAIMS A DAY OF FASTING AND PRAYER, 1798

In 1798, tensions between France and the United States had reached a boiling point, and looked likely to result in war. In the midst of the crisis, John Adams called on Congress to begin preparing for the nation's defense against the French, and he also followed Washington's precedent and called Americans to observe a day of "solemn humiliation, fasting, and prayer."

John Adams, *By the President of the United States* (Philadelphia, 1798), broadside.

By the President of the United States of America,

A PROCLAMATION.

As the safety and prosperity of nations ultimately and essentially depend on the protection and the blessing of Almighty God; and the national acknowledgment of this truth is not only an indispensable duty which the People owe to Him, but a duty whose natural influence is favorable to the promotion of that Morality and Piety, without which social Happiness cannot exist nor the Blessings of a Free Government be enjoyed; and as this Duty, at all times incumbent, is so especially in seasons of Difficulty or of Danger, when existing or threatening Calamities, the just Judgments of God against prevalent Iniquity, are a loud call to Repentance and Reformation: And as the United States of America are, at present, placed in a hazardous and afflictive situation, by the unfriendly Disposition, Conduct and Demands of a foreign power, evinced by repeated refusals to receive our Messengers of Reconciliation and Peace, by Depredations on our Commerce, and the Infliction of Injuries on very many of our Fellow-Citizens, while engaged in their lawful Business on the Seas:—Under these considerations it has appeared to me that the Duty of imploring the Mercy and Benediction of Heaven on our Country demands, at this time, a special attention from its Inhabitants.

I have therefore thought fit to recommend, and I do hereby recommend, that *Wednesday the Ninth Day of May* next be observed throughout the United States, as a day of Solemn Humiliation, Fasting, and Prayer: That the Citizens of these States, abstaining on that Day from their customary Worldly Occupations, offer their devout Addresses to the Father of Mercies, agreeably to those forms or methods which they have severally adopted as the most suitable and becoming: That all Religious Congregations do, with the deepest Humility, acknowledge before God the manifold Sins and Transgressions with which we are justly chargeable as Individuals and as a Nation; beseeching him, at the same time, of his infinite Grace, through the Redeemer of the World, freely to remit all our Offences, and to incline us, by his Holy Spirit, to that sincere Repentance and Reformation which may afford us reason to hope for his inestimable Favour and Heavenly Benediction: That it be made the subject of particular and earnest supplication, that our Country may be protected from all the dangers which threaten it; that our Civil and Religious privileges may be preserved inviolate and perpetuated to the latest Generations; that our public Councils and Magistrates may be especially enlightened and directed at this critical period; that the American People may be united in those Bonds of Amity and mutual Confidence, and inspired with that Vigour and Fortitude by which they have in times past been so highly distinguished, and by which they have obtained such invaluable Advantages: That the Health of the Inhabitants of our Land may be preserved, and their Agriculture,

Commerce, Fisheries, Arts, and Manufactures be blessed and prospered; that the principles of Genuine Piety and Sound Morality may influence the Minds and govern the Lives of every description of our Citizens; and that the Blessings of Peace, Freedom, and Pure Religion, may be speedily extended to all the Nations of the Earth.

And finally I recommend, that on the said day, the Duties of Humiliation and Prayer be accompanied by fervent Thanksgiving to the Bestower of every Good Gift, not only for having hitherto protected and preserved the People of these United States in the independent Enjoyment of their Religious and Civil Freedom, but also for having prospered them in a wonderful progress of Population, and for conferring on them many and great Favours conducive to the Happiness and Prosperity of a Nation.

Given under my Hand and the Seal of the United States of America, at Philadelphia, this twenty-third day of March, in the Year of Our Lord one thousand seven hundred and ninety-eight, and of the Independence of the said States the twenty-second.

JOHN ADAMS

6. THOMAS JEFFERSON'S FIRST INAUGURAL ADDRESS AS PRESIDENT, 1801

When Thomas Jefferson ran for president in the election of 1800, his Federalist opponents painted him as an infidel whose godlessness would ruin the new republic. One critic called him a "howling atheist." So once Jefferson won the election over John Adams, he had to demonstrate that he hardly intended to inaugurate an atheistic reign of terror, as had been seen in the most extreme phases of the French Revolution in the 1790s. He set a conciliatory tone in this excerpt from his first inaugural address, in which he extolled Americans' diverse yet common faith as one of their most important shared values.

From the *Philadelphia Repository and Weekly Register*, March 14, 1801.

Let us then, with courage and confidence pursue our own federal and republican principles; our attachment to union and representative government. Kindly separated by nature and a wide ocean, from the exterminating havoc of one quarter of the globe; too high minded to endure the degradations of the others; possessing a chosen country, with room enough for our descendants to the thousandth and thousandth generation, entertaining a due sense of our equal right to the use of our own faculties, to the acquisitions of our own industry, to honour and confidence from our fellow-citizens, resulting not from birth, but from our actions and their sense of them, enlightened by a benign religion, professed indeed and practised in various forms, yet all of them inculcating honesty, truth, temperance, gratitude and the love of man, acknowledging and adoring an over-ruling Providence, which by all its dispensations proves that it delights in the happiness of man here, and his greater happiness hereafter; with all these blessings, what more is necessary to make us a happy and a prosperous people? Still one thing more, fellow-citizens—a wise and frugal government, which shall restrain men from injuring one another, shall leave them otherwise free to regulate their own pursuits of industry and improvement, and shall not take from the mouth of labour the bread it has earned. This is the sum of good government; and this is necessary to close the circle of our felicities.

7. TREATY BETWEEN THE UNITED STATES AND THE KASKASKIA INDIANS, 1803

In the eighteenth and nineteenth centuries the U.S. government frequently made treaties with Native Americans. This one was negotiated by future president of the United States William Henry Harrison, who was then territorial governor over the Kaskaskia River Valley in Illinois, where the Kaskaskia Indians lived. It was approved by President Thomas Jefferson and ratified by the U.S. Senate in 1803. The treaty states that the U.S. government would provide financial support for seven years for a Catholic priest to minister to the Kaskaskia Indians, and would also help them build a church.

From Charles J. Kappler, ed., *Indian Affairs: Laws and Treaties*, 7 vols. (Washington, DC, 1903), 2:67–68.

ART. 3. . . . *And whereas*, The greater part of the said tribe have been baptised and received into the Catholic church to which they are much attached, the United States will give annually for seven years one hundred dollars towards the support of a priest of that religion, who will engage to perform for the said tribe the duties of his office and also to instruct as many of their children as possible in the rudiments of literature. And the United States will further give the sum of three hundred dollars to assist the said tribe in the erection of a church. The stipulations made in this and the preceding article, together with the sum of five hundred and eighty dollars, which is now paid or assured to be paid for the said tribe for the purpose of procuring some necessary articles, and to relieve them from debts which they have heretofore contracted, is considered as a full and ample compensation for the relinquishment made to the United States in the first article. . . .

8. DOROTHY RIPLEY REMEMBERS HER SERMON IN THE HOUSE OF REPRESENTATIVES, 1806

Dorothy Ripley is believed to be the first woman to preach a sermon in the U.S. Congress. She was an English missionary who spent thirty years in the United States advocating for prison reform and the rights of slaves. She was also a tireless crusader for Christianity, having preached to numerous congregations throughout the United States. In this passage, written in 1822, Ripley recalls her experience preaching a sermon in the Congress, in which she challenged her audience, which included President Thomas Jefferson and Vice President Aaron Burr, to be better disciples of Jesus Christ.

From Dorothy Ripley, *The Bank of Faith and Works United*, 2nd ed. (Whiby, Yorkshire, UK, 1822), 244–247.

This admirable invitation was given to thy hand-maid, to deliver to Congress. . . . How tranquil didst thou keep my soul when standing in the presence of President, Vice-President, Senators, Representatives, and a crowded audience; who gazed with admiration that I was not embarrassed when I took my subject from thy attracting Voice! the Voice of God!

When I sat down in the Speaker's noble chair, methought, Wisdom adorned me with her spotless Robe of innocence: and I perceived her fetters had become a golden chain or ornament put around my neck, which astonished me so much, that I arose and said by the authority of Wisdom, with meekness and fortitude, "I know that I am standing in the midst of some of the wisest men of this land. . . ." The solemnity of the assembly delighted my soul; but with awful reverence, I felt God was in the midst, when supplicating His Throne of Mercy, for assisting Power, that He might be honoured by those Rulers of the land, who had the direction and government of all the United States of America, at this period, when they were convened together for the purpose.

Henceforth, let songs of gratitude arise to Thee, for the richness of Thy Love which I felt so powerfully, that I thought I was not among living men, but dead statutes, without breath of being. The view I had, was no doubt, a true picture of the souls of all who were not born again, "Born of water and the Spirit":[6] which I am afraid were very few, though worshipping to all appearance among professing Christians, the Living and True God, manifested through Jesus Christ His Son, whom He hath appointed Heir of all things, by whom also He made the Worlds....

Thomas Jefferson the President, appeared no more terror to me, than if I were the Queen of the Nation, and he one of my subjects, ruled by my authority; but it was Wisdom, that adorned my mind, and through the condescension of so noble a Mistress, I was empowered to speak to the honour of God, and not regard the appearance of any man, high or low....

After the meeting was finished, I arose, and rendered that respect due to the assembly, whom I reverenced as the higher powers ordained of God, to govern the affairs of men, and testified, "A lonely path is mine, being a member of no society; and also requested of such who feared the Lord, to remember me in their prayers, as I was going to the Southward, as far as Georgia.

6. John 3:5.

Chapter 5

Disestablishment and the Separation of Church and State

1. WILLIAM LINN OPPOSES THOMAS JEFFERSON'S CANDIDACY FOR PRESIDENT, 1800

The Republican Thomas Jefferson was a marked man in the election of 1800. As he challenged the Federalist incumbent John Adams for the presidency that year, his political enemies attacked his character, his honor, and his religious beliefs. They feared that with a Jefferson presidency, a precedent would be set elevating an infidel to the nation's highest office, thus rending the moral fabric of the nation. They found evidence of impiety in Jefferson's *Notes on the State of Virginia*, a selection of which follows. The second selection is from the Reverend William Linn, a Dutch Reformed clergyman from New York City and one of the first chaplains in the U.S. Congress. In his pamphlet *Serious Considerations on the Election of a President: Addressed to the Citizens of the United States*, Linn argued that it was unwise to elect Jefferson because of his anti-Christian views.

From Thomas Jefferson, *Notes on the State of Virginia* (Richmond, VA, 1853), 170–172; William Linn, *Serious Considerations on the*

Election of a President Addressed to the Citizens of the United States
(Trenton, NJ, 1800), 3–4, 14–16.

Thomas Jefferson, *1781*

This is a summary view of that religious slavery, under which a
people have been willing to remain, who have lavished their lives
and fortunes for the establishment of their civil freedom. The
error seems not sufficiently eradicated, that the operations of the
mind, as well as the acts of the body, are subject to the coercion
of the laws. But our rulers can have authority over such natural
rights only as we have submitted to them. The rights of conscience we never submitted, we could not submit. We are
answerable for them to our God. The legitimate powers of government extend to such acts only as are injurious to others. But it
does me no injury for my neighbor to say there are twenty Gods,
or no God. It neither picks my pocket nor breaks my leg. . . . It is
error alone which needs the support of government. Truth can
stand by itself. Subject opinion to coercion: whom will you make
your inquisitors? Fallible men, men governed by bad passions,
by private as well as public reasons. And why subject it to coercion? To produce uniformity. But is uniformity of opinion desirable? No more than of face and stature. . . . Is uniformity
attainable? Millions of innocent men, women, and children,
since the introduction of Christianity, have been burnt, tortured,
fined, imprisoned; yet we have not advanced one inch towards
uniformity. What has been the effect of coercion? To make one-
half of the world fools, and the other half hypocrites. To support
roguery and error all over the earth. Let us reflect that it is inhab-
ited by a thousand millions of people. That these profess probably a thousand different systems of religion. That ours is but one
of that thousand.

William Linn, *1800*

It is well understood that the Honorable Thomas Jefferson is a candidate for the Chief Magistracy[1] of the United States, and that a number of our citizens will give him all their support. I would not presume to dictate to you who ought to be President, but entreat you to hear with patience my reasons why he ought not.

To the declarations of disinterestedness and sincerity already made, I think it proper to add, that I have no personal resentment whatever against Mr. Jefferson, and that it is with pain I oppose him; that I never was in his company, and would hardly know him; that I honor him as holding a high office in government; that I admire his talents, and feel grateful for the services which he has been instrumental in rendering to his country; and that my objection to his being promoted to the Presidency is founded singly upon his disbelief of the Holy Scriptures; or, in other words, his rejection of the Christian Religion and open profession of Deism.

Notwithstanding the general character of Mr. Jefferson, and the proofs of his Deistical principles which have been partly published, at different times, there are some who still doubt; or, if they admit the truth, are disposed to say that he is no worse than his opponents. . . .

There is another passage in Mr. Jefferson's Notes which requires the most serious attention. In showing that civil rulers ought not to interfere with the rights of conscience, and that the legitimate powers of government extend to such acts only as are injurious to others, he says, "It does me no injury for my neighbor to say there are twenty gods, or no god. It neither picks my pocket, nor breaks my leg." The whole passage is written with a great degree of spirit. It is remarkable for that

1. Presidency.

conciseness, perspicuity and force which characterize the style of Mr. Jefferson. Some have ventured, from the words I have quoted to bring even the charge of atheism against him. This is a high charge, and it becomes us carefully to examine the ground upon which it rests; though the words themselves, their connection, and the design for which they are introduced may be insufficient to support it, yet there are concurrent circumstances to be taken into consideration, and which will fix at least a suspicion. These circumstances are, the general disregard of religious things, the associates at home and correspondents abroad, and the principles maintained in conversation. With these things I am not so well acquainted as many. I shall only mention what passed in conversation between Mr. Jefferson and a gentleman of distinguished talents and services, on the necessity of religion to government. The gentleman insisted that some religious faith and institutions of worship, claiming a divine origin, were necessary to the order and peace of society. Mr. Jefferson said that he differed widely from him, and that "he wished to see a government in which no religious opinions were held, and where the security for property and social order rested entirely upon the force of the laws." Would not this be a nation of Atheists? Is it not natural, after the free declaration of such a sentiment, to suspect the man himself of Atheism? Could one who is impressed with the existence of a God, the Creator, Preserver, and Governor of all things, to whom we are under a law and accountable; and the inseparable connection of this truth with the social order and the eternal happiness of mankind, express himself in this manner.

Putting the most favorable construction upon the words in the Notes, they are extremely reprehensible. Does not the belief influence the practice? How then can it be a matter of indifference what a man believes? The doctrine, that a man's life may be good, let his faith be what it may, is contradictory to reason and the experience of mankind. It is true that a mere opinion of my neighbor will do me no injury. Government cannot regulate or punish it. The right of private opinion is inalienable. But let my neighbor once persuade himself that there is no God, and he will soon pick my pocket, and break, not only my leg but my neck. If there be no God, there is no law; no future account; government then is the ordinance of man only, and we cannot be subject for conscience sake. No colors can paint the horrid effects of such a principle, and the deluge of miseries with which it would overwhelm the human race.

2. GEORGE WASHINGTON ON RELIGIOUS LIBERTY, 1789–1790

George Washington's religious views are shrouded in mystery. Of the thousands of pages that total his public and private correspondence, he says very little about Protestant Christianity, Jesus Christ, or organized religion. Though reared as an Anglican, Washington was eclectic in his worship. Throughout his life he frequently attended Anglican, Quaker, German Reformed, and Presbyterian services. The following letters are remarkable for what they reveal about Washington's religious beliefs. When he penned them in 1789–1790, six states—Massachusetts, Maryland, New Hampshire, New Jersey, Connecticut, and North Carolina—still required public officials to take religious oaths for office. Washington wanted to end that practice by promoting religious liberty for all sects and denominations, not just Protestant Christians. In his letter to these religious leaders, Washington affirmed his commitment to the separation of church and state and confirmed that his administration would be neutral in religious affairs.

From W.W. Abbot and Dorothy Twohig, eds., *The Papers of George Washington: Presidential Series*, 15 vols. (Charlottesville, VA, 1987–), 2:423–424, 6:284–285. Used by permission of the publisher.

George Washington to the United Baptists in Virginia

Gentlemen: [New York, May 10, 1789]

I request that you will accept my best acknowledgements for your congratulation on my appointment to the first office in the nation. The kind manner in which you mention my past conduct equally claims the expression of my gratitude.

After we had, by the smiles of Heaven on our exertions, obtained the object for which we contended, I retired at the conclusion of the war, with an idea that my country would have no farther occasion for my services, and with the intention of never entering again into public life: But when the exigence of my country seemed to require me once more to engage in public affairs, an honest conviction of duty superseded my former resolution, and became my apology for deviating from the happy plan which I had adopted.

If I could have entertained the slightest apprehension that the Constitution framed in the Convention, where I had the honor to preside, might possibly endanger the religious rights of any ecclesiastical Society, certainly I would never have placed my signature to it; and if I could now conceive that the general Government might ever be so administered as to render the liberty of conscience insecure, I beg you will be persuaded that no one would be more zealous than myself to establish effectual barriers against the horrors of spiritual tyranny, and every species of religious persecution—For you, doubtless, remember that I have often expressed my sentiment, that every man, conducting himself as a good citizen, and being accountable to God alone for his religious opinions, ought to be protected in worshipping the Deity according to the dictates of his own conscience.

While I recollect with satisfaction that the religious Society of which you are Members, have been, throughout America, uniformly, and almost unanimously, the firm friends to civil liberty, and the persevering Promoters of our glorious revolution; I cannot hesitate to believe that they will be the faithful Supporters of a free, yet efficient general Government. Under this pleasing expectation I rejoice to assure them that they may rely on my best wishes and endeavors to advance their prosperity.

In the meantime be assured, Gentlemen, that I entertain a proper sense of your fervent supplications to God for my temporal and eternal happiness.

G. Washington

George Washington to the Hebrew
Congregation in Newport, Rhode Island

Gentlemen: [Newport, RI, August 18, 1790]

While I receive, with much satisfaction, your Address replete with expressions of affection and esteem; I rejoice in the opportunity of assuring you, that I shall always retain a grateful remembrance of the cordial welcome I experienced in my visit to Newport, from all classes of Citizens.

The reflection on the days of difficulty and danger which are past is rendered the more sweet, from a consciousness that they are succeeded by days of uncommon prosperity and security.

If we have wisdom to make the best use of the advantages with which we are now favored, we cannot fail, under the just administration of a good Government, to become a great and a happy people.

The Citizens of the United States of America have a right to applaud themselves for having given to mankind examples of an enlarged and liberal policy: a policy worthy of imitation. All possess alike liberty of conscience and immunities of citizenship.

It is now no more that toleration is spoken of, as if it were the indulgence of one class of people that another enjoyed the exercise of their inherent natural rights. For happily the Government of the United States, which gives to bigotry no sanction, to persecution no assistance requires only that they who live under its protection should demean themselves as good citizens, in giving it on all occasions their effectual support.

It would be inconsistent with the frankness of my character not to avow that I am pleased with your favorable opinion of my Administration and fervent wishes for my felicity. May the children of the Stock of Abraham,[2] who dwell in this land, continue to merit and enjoy the good will of the other Inhabitants; while every one shall sit in safety under his own vine and figtree and there shall be none to make him afraid.[3] May the father of all mercies scatter light and not darkness in our paths, and make us all in our several vocations useful here, and in his own due time and way everlastingly happy.

Go: Washington

---

2. Old Testament patriarch and founder of Israel.
3. Micah 4:4.

3. JOHN LELAND AND THE BAPTIST CASE FOR RELIGIOUS LIBERTY, 1791

John Leland was a prominent Baptist minister in Massachusetts and Virginia and political ally of Thomas Jefferson and James Madison. An indefatigable advocate of religious liberty, Leland vigorously opposed established state religions and spent much of his career writing and speaking against the Episcopal church in Virginia and Congregational church in New England. This writing, *The Rights of Conscience Inalienable* (1791), was a sermon published in Connecticut just after Leland visited there in 1790. In it, he relies heavily on Thomas Jefferson's *Notes on the State of Virginia*, echoing his arguments that established religions were a violation of the laws of God.

From John Leland, *The Rights of Conscience Inalienable* (New London, CT, 1791), 7–17.

The question *is*, "Are the Rights of Conscience alienable, or inalienable?"

The word *conscience*, signifies *common science*, a court of judicature which the Almighty has erected in every human breast: a *censor morum*[4] over all his conduct. Conscience will ever judge right, when it is rightly informed; and speak the truth when it understands it. But to advert to the question, "Does a man, upon entering into social compact, surrender his conscience to that society, to be controled by the laws thereof; or can he, in justice, assist in making laws to bind his children's consciences before they are born?" I judge not, for the following reasons.

1. Every man must give an account of himself to God, and therefore every man ought to be at liberty to serve God in that

4. A Latin term meaning one who watches over morals.

way that he can best reconcile it to his conscience. If Government, can answer for Individuals at the day of judgment, let men be controled by it, in religious matters; otherwise, let men be free.

2. It would be sinful for a man to surrender that to man, which is to be kept sacred for God. A man's mind should be always open to conviction; and an honest man will receive that doctrine which appears the best demonstrated: and what is more common than for the best of men to change their minds? Such are the prejudices of the mind, and such the force of tradition, that a man who never alters his mind, is either very weak or very stubborn. How painful then must it be to an honest heart, to be bound to observe the principles of his former belief, after he is convinced of their imbecility? and this ever has, and ever will be the case, while the rights of conscience are considered alienable.

3. But supposing it was right for a man to bind his own conscience, yet surely it is very iniquitous to bind the consciences of his children—to make fetters for them before they are born, is very cruel. And yet such has been the conduct of men in almost all ages, that their children have been bound to believe and worship as their fathers did, or suffer shame, loss, and sometimes life; and at best, to be called dissenters; because they dissent from that which they never joined voluntarily. Such conduct in parents is worse than that of the father of Hannibal, who imposed an oath upon his son, while a child, never to be at peace with the Romans.[5]

4. Finally, religion is a matter between God and individuals: religious opinions of men not being the objects of civil government, nor any ways under its control.

5. Hamilcar Barca was the father of the great Carthaginian military leader Hannibal Barca. Hannibal led the Carthaginian army in 247 BC, at a time when Rome sought to conquer Carthage and other nearby cities.

It has often been observed, by the friends of religious establishment by human laws, that no state can long continue without it; that religion will perish, and nothing but infidelity and atheism prevail.

Are these things facts?—Did not the christian religion prevail during the three first centuries, in a more glorious manner than ever it has since; not only without the aid of law, but in opposition to all the laws of haughty monarchs? And did not religion receive a deadly wound by being fostered in the arms of civil power and regulated by law? These things are so.

From that day to this, we have but a few instances of religious liberty to judge by; for in almost all states, civil rulers (by the instigation of covetous priests) have undertaken to steady the ark of religion, by human laws; but yet we have a few of them, without leaving our own land.

The state of Rhode-Island has stood above 160 years without any religious establishment. The state of New-York never had any. New-Jersey claims the same. Pennsylvania has also stood from its first settlement until now upon a liberal foundation; and if agriculture, the mechanical arts and commerce, have not flourished in these states, equal to any of the states, I judge wrong.

It may further be observed, that all the states now in union, saving two or three in New-England, have no legal force used about religion, in directing its course or supporting its preachers.—And moreover, the federal government is forbidden by the constitution, to make any laws, establishing any kind of religion. If religion cannot stand, therefore, without the aid of law, it is likely to fall soon, in our nation, except in Connecticut and Massachusetts.

To say, that "Religion cannot stand without a state establishment," is not only contrary to fact, (as has been proved already) but is a contradiction in phrase. Religion must have stood a time before any law could have been made about it; and if it did stand almost 300 years without law, it can still stand without it.

The evils of such an establishment are many.

1. Uninspired fallible men make their own opinions tests of orthodoxy, and use their own systems, as Rocrustus[6] used his iron bedstead; to stretch and measure the consciences of all others by.—Where no toleration is granted to non-conformists, either ignorance and superstition prevail, or persecution rages: and if toleration is granted to restricted non-conformists, the minds of men are biassed, to embrace that religion which is favored and pampered by law, (and thereby hypocrisy is nourished) while those who cannot stretch their consciences to believe any thing and every thing in the established creed, are treated with contempt and opprobrious names; and by such means some are pampered to death by largesses, and others confined from doing what good, they otherwise could, by penury. The first lie under a temptation to flatter the ruling party, to continue that form of government, which brings them in the sure bread of idleness; the last to despise that government, and those rulers that oppress them.—The first have their eyes shut to all further light, that would alter the religious machine, the last are always seeking new light, and often fall into enthusiasm. Such are the natural evils of establishment in religion by human laws.

2. Such establishments not only wean and alienate the affections of one from another, on account of the different usages they receive, in their religious sentiments, but are also very impolitic, especially in new countries; for what encouragement can

---

6. A character in Greek mythology who stretched or cut off the arms and legs of guests to fit in his bed.

strangers have to migrate with their arts and wealth into a state, where they cannot enjoy their religious sentiments without exposing themselves to the law? when, at the same time their religious opinions do not lead them to be mutinous. And further, how often have kingdoms and states been greatly weakened by religious tests! In the time of the persecution in France,[7] not less than twenty thousand people fled, for the enjoyment of religious liberty.

3. These establishments, metamorphose the church into a creature, and religion into a principle of state; which has a natural tendency to make men conclude that *bible religion* is nothing but a *trick of state*: hence it is that the greatest part of the well informed in literature are over-run with deism and infidelity; nor is it likely it will ever be much better, while preaching is made a trade of emolument.[8] And if there is no difference between *bible religion* and *state religion*, I shall soon fall into infidelity.

4. There are no two kingdoms or states that establish the same creed or formularies of faith, (which alone proves their debility). In one kingdom a man is condemned for not believing a doctrine that he would be condemned for believing in another kingdom. Both of these establishments cannot be right—but both of them can be, and surely are, wrong.

5. The nature of such establishments, further, is to keep from civil office, the best of men. Good men cannot believe what they cannot believe; and they will not subscribe to what they disbelieve; and take an oath to maintain what they conclude is error: and as the best of men differ in judgment, there may be some of them in any state: their talents and virtue entitle them to fill the

---

7. Probably refers to the revocation of the Edict of Nantes in 1685, which led to fierce persecution of French Protestants.

8. Money earned from work.

most important posts, yet because they differ from the established creed of the state they cannot—will not fill those posts. Whereas villains make no scruple to take any oath.

If these, and many more evils, attend such establishments, What were, and still are the causes that ever there should be a state establishment of religion in any empire, kingdom, or state?

The causes are many;—some of which follow:

1. The love of importance is a general evil. It is natural to men, to dictate for others: they choose to command the bushel and use the whip-row; to have the halter around the necks of others, to hang them at pleasure.

2. An over-fondness for a particular system or sect. This gave rise to the first human establishment of religion, by Constantine the Great. Being converted to the christian system, he established it in the Roman empire, compelled the pagans to submit, and banished the christian hereticks; built fine chapels at public expence, and forced large stipends for the preachers. All this was done out of love to the christian religion; but his love operated inadvertently; for he did the christian church more harm than all the persecuting emperors did. It is said, that in his day, a voice was heard from heaven, saying, "Now is poison spued into the churches." If this voice was not heard, it nevertheless was a truth; for from that day to this, the christian religion has been made a stirrup to mount the steed of popularity, wealth and ambition.

3. To produce uniformity in religion. Rulers often fear that if they leave every man to think, speak and worship as he pleases, that the whole cause will be wrecked in diversity; to prevent which, they establish some standard of orthodoxy, to effect uniformity. But, is uniformity attainable? Millions of men, women and children, have been tortured to death, to produce uniformity, and yet the world has not advanced one inch towards it.

And as long as men live in different parts of the world, have different habits, education and interests, they will be different in judgment, humanly speaking.

Is conformity of sentiments, in matters of religion, essential to the happiness of civil government?—Not at all. Government has no more to do with the religious opinions of men, than it has with the principles of the mathematicks. Let every man speak freely without fear—maintain the principles that he believes—worship according to his own faith, either one God, three Gods, no God, or twenty Gods; and let government protect him in so doing, i.e. see that he meets with no personal abuse or loss of property, for his religious opinions. Instead of discouraging of him with proscriptions, fines, confiscation or death; let him be encouraged, as a free man, to bring forth his arguments and maintain his points with all boldness; then, if his doctrine is false, it will be confuted, and if it is true (tho' ever so novel) let others credit it.

When every man has this liberty, what can he wish for more?—A liberal man asks for nothing more of government.

The duty of magistrates is, not to judge of the divinity or tendency of doctrines; but when those principles break out into overt acts of violence, then to use the civil sword and punish the vagrant for what he has done, and not for the religious phrenzy that he acted from.

It is not supposable, that any established creed contains the whole truth, and nothing but truth;—but supposing it did—which established church has got it? All bigots contend for it:—each society cries out "The temple of the Lord are we." Let one society be supposed to be in possession of the whole—let that society be established by law—the creed of faith that they adopt be consecrated so sacred by government, that the man that disbelieves it must die—let this creed finally prevail over the whole world. I ask what honor *truth* gets by all this? None at all. It is famed of a Prussian, called John the Cicero,[9] that by one oration he reconciled two contending princes, actually in war; but, says the historian, "it was his six thousand horse of battle that had the most persuasive oratory." So when one creed or church prevails over another, being armed with (a coat of mail) law and sword, truth gets no honor by the victory. Whereas if all stand upon one footing, being equally protected by law, as citizens, (not as saints) and one prevails over another by cool investigation and fair argument, then truth gains honor; and men more firmly believe it, than if it was made an essential article of salvation, by law.

Truth disdains the aid of law for its defence—it will stand upon its own merits. The heathens worshipped a goddess, called truth, stark naked; and all human decorations of truth, serve only to destroy her virgin beauty. It is error, and error alone, that needs human support; and whenever men fly to the law or sword to protect their system of religion, and force it upon others, it is evident that they have something in their system that will not bear the light, and stand upon the basis of truth.

4. The common objection, "that the ignorant part of the community are not capacitated to judge for themselves," supports the popish hierarchy, and all protestant as well as Turkish and pagan establishments, in idea.

But is this idea just? Has God chosen many of the wise and learned? Has he not hidden the mystery of gospel truth from them, and revealed it unto babes? Does the world, by wisdom,

9. John Cicero was a fifteenth-century Prussian prince who was named after the famed Roman orator Cicero.

know God? Did many of the rulers believe in Christ when he was upon earth? Were not the learned clergy (the scribes) his most inveterate enemies? Do not great men differ as much as little men in judgment? Have not almost all lawless errors crept into the world through the means of wise men (so called)? Is not a simple man, who makes nature and reason his study, a competent judge of things? Is the bible written (like Caligula's laws) so intricate and high that none but the letter-learned (according to common phrase) can read it? Is not the vision written so plain that he that runs may read it? Do not those who understand the original languages, that the bible was written in, differ as much in judgment as others? Are the identical copies of Matthew, Mark, Luke and John, together with the epistles, in every university, and in the hands of every master of arts? If not, have not the learned to trust to a human transcription, as much as the unlearned have to a translation? If these questions, and others of a like nature, can be confuted—then I will confess that it is wisdom for a conclave of bishops, or a convocation of clergy to frame a system out of the bible, and persuade the legislature to legalize it.—No—. It would be attended with so much expence, pride, domination, cruelty and bloodshed, that let me rather fall into infidelity: for no religion at all, is better than that which is worse than none.

5. The ground work of these establishments of religion is, *clerical influence.* Rulers, being persuaded by the clergy that an establishment of religion by human laws, would promote the knowledge of the gospel, quell religious disputes, prevent heresy, produce uniformity, and finally be advantageous to the state, establish such creeds as are framed by the clergy:—and this they often do the more readily, when they are flattered by the clergy; that if they thus defend the truth, they will become *nursing*

fathers to the church, and merit something considerable for themselves.

What stimulates the clergy to recommend this mode of reasoning is,

1. Ignorance—not being able to confute error by fair argument.

2. Indolence—not being willing to spend any time to confute the heretical.

3. But chiefly covetousness, to get money—for it may be observed that in all these establishments, settled salaries for the clergy, recoverable by law, are sure to be interwoven: and was not this the case, I am well convinced that there would not be many, if any religious establishments, in the christian world.

4. THOMAS JEFFERSON AND THE DANBURY BAPTISTS, 1801–1802

Thomas Jefferson's letter to the Danbury Baptists is one of the most controversial documents in American history. Early in Jefferson's presidential administration, some Danbury Baptists in Connecticut wrote the president requesting his views about religious liberty. Disgruntled that they were a religious minority in a state that supported legal privileges for the Congregational church, the Baptists hoped President Jefferson would support religious liberty for the new nation just as he had done in Virginia. Jefferson's reply, which is a classic in American letters, established for the first time a new metaphor in the American lexicon: the "wall of separation between church and state." That simple phrase became the basis of a new paradigm for religious freedom in the United States—a paradigm that has become increasingly relevant in the past sixty years as judges and politicians have debated the meaning of the First Amendment and the place of religious liberty in a democratic republic.

From *The Bee* (New London, CT), February 3, 1802; *American Mercury* (Hartford, CT), January 28, 1802.

Danbury Baptist Association to Thomas Jefferson

SIR,

AMONG the many millions in America and Europe who rejoice in your election to office, we embrace the first opportunity which we have enjoyed in our collective capacity since your inauguration to express our great satisfaction on your appointment to the chief magistracy in the United States; and though our mode of expression may be less courtly and pompous than what many others clothe their address with, we beg you, sir, to believe that none are more sincere.

Our sentiments are uniformly on the side of religious liberty; that *religion* is at all times and places a matter between God and individuals; that no man ought to suffer in name, person or effects, on account of his religious opinions; that the legitimate power of civil goverment extends no further than to punish the man who *works ill to his neighbour.* But, sir, our constitution of government is not specific. Our ancient charter, together with the laws made under it, were adopted as the basis of our government, at the time of our revolution; and such had been our laws and usages, and such still are, that *religion* is considered as the first object of legislation; and therefore what religious privileges we enjoy (as a minor part of the state) we enjoy as *favors granted,* and not as *inalienable rights*; and these *favors* we receive at the expence of such degrading acknowledgments as are inconsistent with the rights of freemen. It is not to be wondered at, therefore, if these men who seek after *power* and *gain*, under the pretence of *government* and *religion*, should reproach their fellow-men; should reproach their chief magistrate, as an enemy of religion, law and good order, because he will not, does not, assume the prerogatives of JEHOVAH, and make Laws to govern the kingdom of Christ.

Sir, we are sensible that the President of the United States is not the national legislature; and also sensible that the national government cannot destroy the laws of each state; but our hopes are strong, that the sentiments of our beloved President which have had such genial effect already, like the radiant rays of the sun, will shine and prevail through all these states, and all the world, till hierarchy and tyranny be destroyed from the earth. Sir, when we reflect on your past services, and see a glow of philanthropy and good will shining forth in a course of more than *thirty years*, we have reason to believe that America's God has raised you up to fill the chair of state, out of that good will which he bears to the many millions over which you preside. May God strengthen you for the arduous task which Providence and the voice of the people have called you to sustain, and support you against all the *predetermined* opposition of those who wish to rise to wealth and importance on the poverty and subjection of the people. And may the Lord preserve you safe from every evil, and bring you at last to his heavenly kingdom, through Jesus Christ our glorious mediator.

Signed in behalf of the Association,

Nehemiah Dodge, Ephraim Robbins,

Stephen S. Nelson, Committee.

Thomas Jefferson to the Danbury Baptist Association

Gentlemen,

The affectionate sentiments of esteem and approbation which you are so good as to express towards me, on behalf of the Danbury Baptist association, give me the highest satisfaction; my duties dictate a faithful and zealous pursuit of the interests of my constituents and in proportion as they are persuaded of my fidelity to those duties the discharge of them becomes more and more pleasing.

Believing with you, that religion is a matter which lies solely between man and his God, that he owes account to none other for his faith or his worship, that the legislative[10] powers of government reach actions only, and not opinions, I contemplate with sovereign reverence that act of the whole American people which declared that *their* legislature should "make no law respecting an establishment of religion, or prohibiting the free exercise thereof;" thus building a wall of separation between church and state. Adhering to this expression of the supreme will of the nation, in behalf of the rights of conscience, I shall see with sincere satisfaction the progress of those sentiments which tend to restore to man all his natural rights, convinced he has no natural right in opposition to his social duties.

I reciprocate your kind prayers for the protection and blessing of the common father and creator of man, and tender you, for yourselves and your religious association, assurances of my high respect and esteem.

THOMAS JEFFERSON

January 1, 1802.

---

10. Jefferson's original letter said "legitimate" instead of "legislative."

5. THOMAS JEFFERSON REFUSES TO DECLARE DAYS OF PRAYER AND FASTING, 1808

In this revealing letter, President Jefferson explains why he did not have the authority to issue "a day of fasting and prayer." He deemed religion a responsibility of the states, and he did not think that the "General Government" had any control over such matters. In advancing this interpretation, Jefferson broke from his predecessors, George Washington and John Adams, who frequently called for days of fasting and prayer during their administrations.

From Thomas Jefferson to Reverend Samuel Miller, January 23, 1808, in *The Writings of Thomas Jefferson*, ed. Andrew A. Lipscomb and Albert Ellery Bergh, 20 vols. (Washington, DC, 1903), 11:428–430.

Letter from Thomas Jefferson to the Reverend Samuel Miller (January 23, 1808)

Sir,—I have duly received your favor of the 18th, and am thankful to you for having written it, because it is more agreeable to prevent than to refuse what I do not think myself authorized to comply with. I consider the government of the United States as interdicted[11] by the Constitution from intermeddling with religious institutions, their doctrines, discipline, or exercises. This results not only from the provision that no law shall be made respecting the establishment or free exercise of religion,[12] but from that also which reserves to the States the powers not delegated to the United States.[13] Certainly, no power to prescribe any religious exercise, or

11. Prohibited or forbidden.
12. First Amendment of the U.S. Constitution.
13. Tenth Amendment of the U.S. Constitution.

to assume authority in religious discipline, has been delegated to the General Government. It must then rest with the States, as far as it can be in any human authority. But it is only proposed that I should *recommend*, not prescribe a day of fasting and prayer. That is, that I should *indirectly* assume to the United States an authority over religious exercises, which the Constitution has directly precluded them from. It must be meant, too, that this recommendation is to carry some authority, and to be sanctioned by some penalty on those who disregard it; not indeed of fine and imprisonment, but of some degree of proscription, perhaps in public opinion. And does the change in the nature of the penalty make the recommendation the less a *law* of conduct for those to whom it is directed? I do not believe it is for the interest of religion to invite the civil magistrate[14] to direct its exercises, its discipline, or its doctrines; nor of the religious societies, that the General Government should be invested with the power of effecting any uniformity of time or matter among them. Fasting and prayer are religious exercises; the enjoining them an act of discipline. Every religious society has a right to determine for itself the times for these exercises, and the objects proper for them, according to their own particular tenets; and this right can never be safer than in their own hands, where the Constitution has deposited it.

I am aware that the practice of my predecessors may be quoted. But I have ever believed, that the example of State executives led to the assumption of that authority by the General Government, without due examination, which would have discovered that what might be a right in a State government, was a violation of that right when assumed by another. Be this as it may, every one must act according to the dictates of his own

14. A judicial officer such as a judge.

reason, and mine tells me that civil powers alone have been given to the President of the United States and no authority to direct the religious exercises of his constituents.

I again express my satisfaction that you have been so good as to give me an opportunity of explaining myself in a private letter, in which I could give my reasons more in detail than might have been done in a public answer; and I pray you to accept the assurances of my high esteem and respect.

6. JOHN ADAMS ON THE "NATIONAL GOVERNMENT MEDDLING WITH RELIGION," 1812

John Adams was a bitter man when Thomas Jefferson defeated him for the presidency in 1800. Twelve years later he wrote a poignant letter to his friend and confidante, Benjamin Rush, explaining that his presidential appointment of a day for "humiliation, fasting, and prayer" had been used against him by political opponents. They depicted him as a supporter of an established church, a point Adams energetically disputed. As he explained to Rush in this letter, "Nothing is more dreaded than the national government meddling with religion."

From John Adams to Benjamin Rush, June 12, 1812, in *The Spur of Fame: Dialogues of John Adams and Benjamin Rush, 1805–1813*, ed. John A. Schutz and Douglass Adair (San Marino, CA, 1966), 224. Used by permission of the Henry E. Huntington Library.

Dear Sir, June 12, 1812

. . . I agree with you, there is a germ of religion in human nature so strong that whenever an order of men can persuade the people by flattery or terror that they have salvation at their disposal, there can be no end to fraud, violence, or usurpation. Ecumenical councils produce ecumenical bishops, and both, subservient armies, emperors, and kings.

The national fast recommend by me turned me out of office. It was connected with the General Assembly of the Presbyterian Church which I had no concern in. That Assembly has alarmed and alienated Quakers, Anabaptists, Mennonites, Moravians, Swedenborgians, Methodists, Catholics, Protestant Episcopalians, Arians, Socinians, Arminians, etc., . . . A general suspicion prevailed that the Presbyterian Church was ambitious and aimed at an establishment as a national church. I was represented as a Presbyterian and at the head of this political and ecclesiastical project. The secret whisper ran through all the sects, "Let us have Jefferson, Madison, Burr,[15] anybody, whether they be philosophers, Deists, or even atheists, rather than a Presbyterian President." This principle is at the bottom of the unpopularity of national fasts and thanksgivings. Nothing is more dreaded than the national government meddling with religion. This wild letter, I very much fear, contains seeds of an ecclesiastical history of the U.S. for a century to come.

John Adams

15. Aaron Burr.

Chapter 6

The Founding Fathers' Own
Views on Religion

1. THOMAS JEFFERSON, 1787, 1803

No Founder's views on religion have been more studied and debated than Thomas Jefferson's. Jefferson kept quiet for much of his career about his own theology, apparently assuming that airing his views would not help him politically. Opinions shared later confirmed that Jefferson was a person of unorthodox beliefs. But, despite some accusations, Jefferson was no atheist. He believed in God, and believed that Jesus was the greatest moral teacher in history. But he was deeply skeptical about institutional Christianity, and the accretion of theology about Jesus over the centuries. He particularly doubted the idea that Jesus was God, that God existed as Trinity (Father, Son, and Holy Spirit), and that Jesus rose from the dead. After his political career was over, Jefferson produced an edition of the New Testament with the miracles and resurrection of Christ removed. All that remained were Jesus's moral teachings.

The following two selections help clarify Jefferson's religious views. In the first, a 1787 letter to his nephew Peter Carr, Jefferson insists that Carr should question traditional theology, and should read the Bible as a historical document, rather than as a divine text. In the second, an 1803 letter to fellow patriot leader Benjamin Rush,

Jefferson explains his devotion to the teachings of the actual Jesus of history. He also reflects on his reluctance to share his religious views with the public.

From Paul Leicester Ford, ed., *The Works of Thomas Jefferson* (New York, 1904), 5:324–327; 9:457–458.

To Peter Carr *August 10, 1787*

. . . Religion. Your reason is now mature enough to examine this object. In the first place divest yourself of all bias in favor of novelty and singularity of opinion. Indulge them in any other subject rather than that of religion. It is too important, and the consequences of error may be too serious. On the other hand shake off all the fears and servile prejudices under which weak minds are servilely crouched. Fix reason firmly in her seat, and call to her tribunal every fact, every opinion. Question with boldness even the existence of a god; because, if there be one, he must more approve of the homage of reason, than that of blindfolded fear. You will naturally examine first the religion of your own country. Read the bible then, as you would read Livy or Tacitus.[1] The facts which are within the ordinary course of nature you will believe on the authority of the writer, as you do those of the same kind in Livy and Tacitus. The testimony of the writer weighs in their favor in one scale, and their not being against the laws of nature does not weigh against them. But those facts in the bible which contradict the laws of nature, must be examined with more care, and under a variety of faces. Here you must recur to the pretensions of the writer to inspiration from god. Examine upon what evidence his pretensions are founded, and whether

1. Historians in ancient Rome.

that evidence is so strong as that its falsehood would be more improbable than a change in the laws of nature in the case he relates. For example in the book of Joshua we are told the sun stood still several hours. Were we to read that fact in Livy or Tacitus we should class it with their showers of blood, speaking of statutes, beasts, [etc.] But it is said that the writer of that book was inspired. Examine therefore candidly what evidence there is of his having been inspired. The pretension is entitled to your inquiry, because millions believe it. On the other hand you are astronomer enough to know how contrary it is to the law of nature that a body revolving on its axis as the earth does, should have stopped, should not by that sudden stoppage have prostrated animals, trees, buildings, and should after a certain time have resumed its revolution, and that without a second general prostration. Is this arrest of the earth's motion, or the evidence which affirms it, most within the law of probabilities? You will next read the new testament. It is the history of a personage called Jesus. Keep in your eye the opposite pretensions 1. of those who say he was begotten by god, born of a virgin, suspended and reversed the laws of nature at will, and ascended bodily into heaven: and 2. of those who say he was a man of illegitimate birth, of a benevolent heart, enthusiastic mind, who set out without pretensions to divinity, ended in believing them, and was punished capitally for sedition by being gibbeted according to the Roman law which punished the first commission of that offence by whipping, and the second by exile or death . . .

Do not be frightened from this inquiry by any fear of its consequences. If it ends in a belief that there is no god, you will find incitements to virtue in the comfort and pleasantness you feel in its exercise, and the love of others which it will procure you. If you find reason to believe there is a god, a consciousness that you are acting under his eye, and that he approves you, will be a vast additional incitement; if that there be a future state, the hope of a happy existence in that increases the appetite to deserve it; if that Jesus was also a god, you will be comforted by a belief of his aid and love. In fine, I repeat that you must lay aside all prejudice on both sides, and neither believe nor reject anything because any other persons, or description of persons have rejected or believed it. Your own reason is the only oracle given you by heaven, and you are answerable not for the rightness but uprightness of the decision. I forgot to observe when speaking of the new testament that you should read all the histories of Christ, as well of those whom a council of ecclesiastics have decided for us to be Pseudo-evangelists,[2] as those they named Evangelists. Because these Pseudo-evangelists pretended to inspiration as much as the others, and you are to judge their pretensions by your own reason, and not by the reason of those ecclesiastics. Most of these are lost. There are some however still extant, collected by Fabricius which I will endeavor to get and send you.

To Benjamin Rush *April 21, 1803*

Dear Sir,—In some of the delightful conversations with you, in the evenings of 1798–99, and which served as an anodyne to the afflictions of the crisis through which our country was then laboring, the Christian religion was sometimes our topic; and I then promised you, that one day or other, I would give you my views of it. They are the result of a life of inquiry & reflection, and very different from that anti-Christian system imputed to me by those who know nothing of my opinions. To the corruptions of

---

2. Ancient authors of gospels, or histories of Jesus, other than the four canonical authors (Matthew, Mark, Luke, and John).

Christianity I am indeed opposed; but not to the genuine precepts of Jesus himself. I am a Christian, in the only sense he wished any one to be; sincerely attached to his doctrines, in preference to all others; ascribing to himself every *human* excellence; & believing he never claimed any other. At the short intervals since these conversations, when I could justifiably abstract my mind from public affairs, the subject has been under my contemplation. But the more I considered it, the more it expanded beyond the measure of either my time or information. In the moment of my late departure from Monticello, I received from Doctr Priestley,[3] his little treatise of *Socrates & Jesus compared.* This being a section of the general view I had taken of the field it became a subject of reflection while on the road, and unoccupied otherwise. The result was, to arrange in my mind a syllabus, or outline of such an estimate of the comparative merits of Christianity, as I wished to see executed by some one of more leisure and information for the task, than myself. This I now send you,[4] as the only discharge of my promise I can probably ever execute. And in confiding it to you, I know it will not be exposed to the malignant perversions of those who make every word from me a text for new misrepresentations & calumnies. I am moreover averse to the communication of my religious tenets to the public; because it would countenance the presumption of those who have endeavored to draw them before that tribunal, and to seduce public opinion to erect itself into that inquisition over the rights of conscience, which the laws have so justly proscribed. It behoves every man who values liberty of conscience for himself, to resist invasions of it in the case of others; or their case may, by

3. Joseph Priestley, a British theologian and scientist who frequently corresponded with Jefferson.
4. Jefferson attached a "syllabus" regarding the superiority of Jesus's moral teachings.

change of circumstances, become his own. It behoves him, too, in his own case, to give no example of concession, betraying the common right of independent opinion, by answering questions of faith, which the laws have left between God & himself. Accept my affectionate salutations.

2. JOHN ADAMS, 1810, 1813

In a bitter national election in 1800, Thomas Jefferson defeated his archenemy John Adams, the sitting president. Despite their deep political disagreements, they shared similar doubts about traditional Christian doctrine. As seen in the 1813 letter here, in their retirement years Adams and Jefferson confided their views to one another on many issues, including religion.

Adams grew up in a traditional Congregationalist family in Massachusetts, which was still heavily influenced by the colony's Puritan heritage. Adams slowly gravitated toward a more liberal form of Christianity, however. In addition to questioning the reliability of the Bible, Adams particularly questioned the doctrine of the Trinity and the Calvinist beliefs of his youth, including predestination.

In the letters that follow, one sees Adams's combination of devotion and skepticism regarding Christianity. In the first letter, written to Benjamin Rush, a friend of both Adams and Jefferson, Adams expresses his admiration for the one true God of Christianity and his disdain for theological squabbles of the denominations. In the second letter, written to Jefferson in 1813, Adams shows his raging contempt for Trinitarian and Calvinist Christianity.

John Adams to Benjamin Rush, January 21, 1810, in *The Works of John Adams*, ed. Charles F. Adams (Boston, 1854), 9:627; John

Adams to Thomas Jefferson, September 14, 1813, in *Works of John Adams*, ed. Adams, 10:66–67.

To Benjamin Rush *January 21, 1810*

. . . The Christian religion, as I understand it, is the brightness of the glory and the express portrait of the character of the eternal, self-existent, independent, benevolent, all powerful and all merciful creator, preserver, and father of the universe, the first good, first perfect, and first fair. It will last as long as the world. Neither savage nor civilized man, without a revelation, could ever have discovered or invented it. Ask me not, then, whether I am Catholic or Protestant, Calvinist or Arminian.[5] As far as they are Christians, I wish to be a fellow-disciple with them all.

To Thomas Jefferson *September 14, 1813*

. . . We can never be so certain of any prophecy, or the fulfillment of any prophecy, or of any miracle, or the design of any miracle, as we are from the revelation of nature, that is, nature's God, that two and two are equal to four. Miracles or prophecies might frighten us out of our wits, might scare us to death, might induce us to lie, to say that we believe that two and two make five, but we should not believe it; we should know the contrary.

Had you and I been forty days with Moses on Mount Sinai, and admitted to behold the divine Shechinah,[6] and there told that one was three and three one, we might not have had courage to deny it, but we could not have believed it. The thunders and lightnings and earthquakes, and the transcendent splendors and glories, might have overwhelmed us with terror and amazement, but we could not have believed the doctrine. We should be more

5. Calvinists and Arminians debated the role of human free will in salvation.
6. Exodus 24:16–18.

likely to say in our hearts—whatever we might say with our lips—, This is chance. There is no God, no truth. This is all delusion, fiction, and a lie, or it is all chance . . .

Now, my friend, can prophecies or miracles convince you or me that infinite benevolence, wisdom, and power, created, and preserves for a time, innumerable millions, to make them miserable forever,[7] for his own glory? Wretch! What is his glory? Is he ambitious? Does he want promotion? Is he vain, tickled with adulation, exulting and triumphing in his power and the sweetness of his vengeance? Pardon me, my Maker, for these awful questions. My answer to them is always ready. I believe no such things. My adoration of the author of the universe is too profound and too sincere. The love of God and his creation— delight, joy, triumph, exultation in my own existence—though but an atom, a *molécule organique* in the universe—are my religion.

Howl, snarl, bite, ye Calvinistic, ye Athanasian[8] divines, if you will; ye will say I am no Christian; I say ye are no Christians, and there the account is balanced. Yet I believe all the honest men among you are Christians, in my sense of the word.

3. BENJAMIN FRANKLIN, 1771, 1790

Like John Adams, Benjamin Franklin grew up in a conservative Congregationalist family in Massachusetts. But by his teenage years, Franklin began to read Deist writers from England, and became

7. In hell.
8. Athanasius was a fourth-century CE Christian theologian who argued for the divinity of Jesus.

convinced that traditional Christianity was corrupt and deficient. Franklin never became an activist for Deism—that was not his style. Instead, Franklin handled his religious beliefs lightly, believing that his primary obligation was to live out his beliefs, rather than to profess correct doctrines. Therefore, Franklin felt comfortable befriending the leading evangelical revivalist of the age, George Whitefield. He also seemed to endorse stronger views of Providence and the efficacy of prayer than one might expect of a Deist, such as when Franklin proposed that the Constitutional Convention begin its daily business with prayer. But still, it seems clear that when compared to the other top-rank Founding Fathers, Franklin and Jefferson were probably the most skeptical about traditional Christianity. Like Jefferson, Franklin's religion was one of reason and morality, not revelation.

In the first selection excerpted here, Franklin writes in his *Autobiography* about his decision to become a Deist. In the second, Franklin explained his "creed" to Yale College president Ezra Stiles.

From Benjamin Franklin, *Autobiography*, in *Memoirs of Benjamin Franklin* (New York, 1859), 1:23, 33; Benjamin Franklin to Ezra Stiles, March 9, 1790, in *Autobiography*, 1:622–623.

Before I enter upon my public appearance in business, it may be well to let you know the then state of my mind, with regard to my principles and morals, that you may see how far those influenced the future events of my life. My parents had early given me religious impressions, and brought me through my childhood piously in the dissenting way. But I was scarce fifteen, when, after doubting by turns of several points, as I found them disputed in the different books I read, I began to doubt of the revelation itself. Some books against Deism fell into my hands—they were said to be the substance of the sermons which had been preached at Boyle's lectures.[9] It happened that they wrought an effect on me quite contrary to what was intended by them; for the arguments of the Deists which were quoted to be refuted appeared to me much stronger than the refutations; in short, I soon became a thorough Deist . . .

I had been religiously educated as a Presbyterian; but though some of the dogmas of that persuasion, such as *the eternal decrees of God, election, reprobation,* [etc.] appeared to me unintelligible, and I early absented myself from the public assemblies of the sect, (Sunday being my studying day.) I never was without some religious principles: I never doubted, for instance, the existence of a Deity, that he made the world, and governed it by his providence; that the most acceptable service of God was the doing good to man; that our souls are immortal; and that all crimes will be punished, and virtue rewarded, either here or hereafter; these I esteemed the essentials of every religion, and being to be found in all the religions we had in our country, I respected them all, though with different degrees of respect, as I found them more or less mixed with other articles, which, without any tendency to inspire, promote, or confirm morality, served principally to divide us, and make us unfriendly to one another. This respect to all, with an opinion that the worst had some [good] effects, induced me to avoid all discourse that might tend to lessen the good opinion another might have of his own religion; and as our province increased in people, and new places of worship were continually wanted, and generally erected by voluntary contribution, my mite for such purpose, whatever might be the sect, was never refused.

9. A series of lectures given annually in Britain to defend Christianity.

Though I seldom attended any public worship, I had still an opinion of its propriety, and of its utility when rightly conducted, and I regularly paid my annual subscription for the support of the only Presbyterian minister or meeting we had in Philadelphia. He used to visit me sometimes as a friend, and admonish me to attend his administrations; and I was now and then prevailed on to do so; once for five Sundays successively. Had he been in my opinion a good preacher, perhaps I might have continued, notwithstanding the occasion I had for the Sunday's leisure in my course of study: but his discourses were chiefly either polemic arguments, or explications of the peculiar doctrines of our sect, and were all to me very dry, uninteresting, and unedifying, since not a single moral principle was inculcated or enforced; their aim seeming to be rather to make us *Presbyterians*, than *good citizens*. At length he took for his text that verse of the fourth chapter to the Philippians, "*Finally, brethren, whatsoever things are true, honest, just, pure, lovely, or of good report, if there be any virtue, or any praise, think on these things.*" And I imagined in a sermon on such a text, we could not miss of having some morality. But he confined himself to five points only, as meant by the apostle, viz.[10] 1. Keeping holy the Sabbath day; 2. Being diligent in reading the holy Scriptures; 3. Attending duly the public worship; 4. Partaking of the sacrament; 5. Paying a due respect to God's ministers. These might be all good things, but as they were not the kind of good things that I expected from that text, I despaired of ever meeting with them from any other, was disgusted, and attended his preaching no more. I had some years before composed a little liturgy, or form of prayer, for my own private use, (viz. in 1728,) entitled, *Articles of Belief and Acts of*

10. That is.

Religion. I returned to the use of this, and went no more to the public assemblies. My conduct might be blameable, but I leave it without attempting further to excuse it; my present purpose being to relate facts, and not to make apologies for them.

To Ezra Stiles *March 9, 1790*

You desire to know something of my religion. It is the first time I have been questioned upon it. But [I] cannot take your curiosity amiss, and shall endeavour in a few words to gratify it. Here is my creed: I believe in one God, the creator of the universe. That he governs it by his Providence. That he ought to be worshipped. That the most acceptable service we render to him is doing good to his other children. That the soul of man is immortal, and will be treated with justice in another life respecting its conduct in this. These I take to be the fundamental points in all sound religion, and I regard them as you do in whatever sect I meet with them. As to Jesus of Nazareth, my opinion of whom you particularly desire, I think the system of morals and his religion, as he left them to us, the best the world ever saw or is like to see; but I apprehend, it has received various corrupting changes, and I have, with most of the present dissenters[11] in England, some doubts as to his divinity; though it is a question I do not dogmatize upon, having never studied it, and think it needless to busy myself with it now, when I expect soon an opportunity of knowing the truth with less trouble. I see no harm, however, in its being believed, if that belief has the good consequence, as probably it has, of making his doctrines more respected and more observed, especially as I do not perceive that the Supreme takes it amiss by

11.Non-Anglicans, or those outside the established state church.

distinguishing the believers in his government of the world with any peculiar marks of his displeasure. I shall only add respecting myself, that having experienced the goodness of that Being in conducting me prosperously through a long life, I have no doubt of its continuance in the next, though without the smallest conceit of meriting such goodness . . .

4. THOMAS PAINE, 1776

Thomas Paine was the most influential polemical writer of the American Revolution. His pamphlet *Common Sense* (1776) caused a sensation in the colonies and helped prepare Americans for their final break with Britain. Although Paine had a background in both Quakerism and Methodism, by the time of the Revolution he had begun to gravitate toward Deism. In 1791, Paine went to France to support the French Revolution, but when the radical Jacobins seized control of the Revolution in 1794, Paine was imprisoned and nearly executed. Prior to his imprisonment, Paine wrote *The Age of Reason*, a treatise against traditional, institutional religion. In it, he denied most of the key doctrines of Christianity, including Jesus's divinity, the virgin birth, and the resurrection. *The Age of Reason* found an eager audience in America, where seventeen editions appeared between 1794 and 1796. The book also generated a backlash against Paine, who was widely denounced for having betrayed the godly spirit of the American Revolution. In this excerpt, Paine explains his personal beliefs and individualistic view of religion.

From Thomas Paine, *The Age of Reason* (New York, 1827), 5–7.

I believe in one God, and no more: and I hope for happiness beyond this life.

I believe [in] the equality of man; and I believe that religious duties consist in doing justice, loving mercy, and endeavoring to make our fellow creatures happy.

But, lest it should be supposed that I believe many other things in addition to these, I shall, in the progress of this work, declare the things I do not believe, and my reasons for not believing them.

I do not believe in the creed professed by the Jewish church, by the Roman church, by the Greek church, by the Turkish church, by the Protestant church, nor by any church that I know of. My own mind is my own church.

All national institutions of churches whether Jewish, Christian or Turkish, appear to me no other than human inventions, set up to terrify and enslave mankind, and monopolize power and profit . . .

Soon after I had published the pamphlet "Common Sense," in America, I saw the exceeding probability that a revolution in the system of government would be followed by a revolution in the system of religion. The adulterous connection of church and state, wherever it had taken place, whether Jewish, Christian or Turkish, had so effectually prohibited by pains and penalties every discussion upon established creeds, and upon first principles of religion, that until the system of government should be changed, those principles could not be brought fairly and openly before the world; but that whenever this should be done, a revolution in the system of religion would follow. Human inventions and priestcraft would be detected; and man would return to the pure, unmixed, and unadulterated belief of one God, and no more.

Every national church or religion has established itself by pretending some special mission from God, communicated to certain individuals. The Jews have their Moses; the Christians their Jesus Christ, their apostles and saints; and the Turks their Mahomet, as if the way to God was not open to every man alike. Each of these churches show certain books, which they call revelation or the word of God. The Jews say, that their word of God was given by God to Moses, face to face; the Christians say, that their word of God came by divine inspiration; and the Turks say, that their word of God (the Koran) was brought by an angel from heaven. Each of these churches accuse the other of unbelief; and for my own part, I disbelieve them all.

5. PATRICK HENRY, 1796

Thomas Paine and Patrick Henry had been at the forefront of the movement for independence in the 1770s. But on the role of religion in society, they could not have been more different. Henry was a traditional Anglican (or Episcopalian, after the Revolution) and apparently became even more devout in his later years. Part of the reason for his increasing concern for Christianity was Paine and *The Age of Reason*. Henry had assumed that the new American republic would be sustained by virtue, which naturally came from religious sources. But as Paine gained more of an audience in the 1790s, Henry insisted that turning against Christianity represented a betrayal of the Revolution. In this letter to his daughter, Henry reflects on the threat of Deism in America. The letter was published repeatedly in American newspapers for decades after Henry's death in 1799.

Patrick Henry to Elizabeth Aylett, August 20, 1796, in *Patrick Henry: Life, Correspondence, and Speeches*, ed. William Wirt Henry (New York, 1891), 2:570–571.

To Elizabeth Aylett *August 20, 1796*

. . . The view which the rising greatness of our country presents to my eye is greatly tarnished by the general prevalence of deism; which with me, is but another name for vice and depravity. I am, however, much consoled by reflecting, that the religion of Christ has, from its first appearance in the world, been attacked in vain by all the wits, philosophers, and wise ones aided by every power of man, and its triumph has been complete. What is there in the wit or wisdom of the present deistical writers or professors, that can compare them with Hume, Shaft[e]sbury, Bolingbroke,[12] and others? And yet these have been confuted, and their fame decaying; insomuch that the puny efforts of Paine are thrown in to prop their tottering fabric, whose foundations cannot stand the test of time. Amongst other strange things said of me, I hear it is said by the deists that I am one of their number; and indeed, that some good people think I am no Christian. This thought gives me much more pain than the appellation of tory;[13] because I think religion of infinitely higher importance than politics; and I find much cause to reproach myself that I have lived so long and have given no decided proofs of my being a Christian. But, indeed, my dear child, this is a character I prize far above all this world has or can boast. And amongst all the handsome things I hear said of you, what gives me the greatest pleasure is to be told of your piety and steady virtue.

---

12. David Hume, Lord Shaftesbury, and Henry St. John Bolingbroke were British writers who had all expressed doubts about traditional Christian doctrine, and were often considered Deists.
13. A British Loyalist.

6. SAMUEL ADAMS, 1780, 1802

Like his cousin John, Samuel Adams grew up in a conservative Congregationalist family in Massachusetts. Unlike John, Samuel essentially maintained that faith throughout his career. Like Patrick Henry, Adams was one of the early radicals pushing for independence from Britain, and he also assumed that the new American republic would be rooted in Christian virtue. Signs that the people might be turning away from faith and virtue, for Adams, heralded danger to liberty. Liberty must be channeled toward benevolent purposes, he believed, or it risked becoming an excuse for immoral chaos.

In the first selection that follows, Adams explains the intimate connection he saw between virtue and liberty and expresses hope that his native Boston could become a "Christian Sparta." In the second letter, written shortly before his death, Adams vents his anger directly against Thomas Paine for promoting irreligion.

Samuel Adams to John Scollay, December 30, 1780, in *The Writings of Samuel Adams*, ed. Harry Alonzo Cushing (New York, 1908), 4:236–238; Samuel Adams to Thomas Paine, November 30, 1802, in *Writings of Samuel Adams*, 4:412–413.

To John Scollay *December 30, 1780*

Our Government, I perceive, is organizd on the Basis of the new Constitution. I am affraid there is more Pomp & Parade than is consistent with those sober Republican Principles, upon which the Framers of it thought they had founded it. Why should this new Era be introducd with Entertainments expensive & tending to dissipate the Minds of the People? Does it become us to lead the People to such publick Diversions as promote Superfluity of Dress & Ornament, when it is as much as they can bear to support the Expense of cloathing a naked Army? Will Vanity & Levity ever be the Stability of Government, either in States, in Cities, or what, let me hint to you is of the last Importance, in *Families?* Of what Kind are those Manners, by which, as we are truly informd in a late Speech, "not only the freedom but the very Existence of Republicks is greatly affected?" How fruitless is it, to recommend "the adapting the Laws in the most perfect Manner possible, to the Suppression of Idleness Dissipation & Extravagancy," if such Recommendations are counteracted by the Example of Men of Religion, Influence & publick Station? I meant to consider this Subject in the View of the mere Citizen. But I have mentiond the sacred Word *Religion.* I confess, I am surprizd to hear, that some particular Persons have been so unguarded as to give their Countenance to such kind of Amusements. I wish Mr—would recollect his former Ideas when his Friend Whit[e]field[14] thunderd in the Pulpit against Assemblies & Balls . . .

But I fear I shall say too much. I love the People of Boston. I once thought, that City would be the *Christian* Sparta. But Alas! Will men never be free! They will be free no longer than while they remain virtuous. Sidney[15] tells us, there are times when People are not worth saving. Meaning, when they have lost their Virtue. I pray God, this may never be truly said of my beloved Town.

---

14. George Whitefield was the leading preacher of the First Great Awakening in America and Britain.
15. Algernon Sidney was a seventeenth-century English political theorist.

To Thomas Paine *November 30, 1802*

SIR,—

I have frequently with pleasure reflected on your services to *my* native and *your* adopted country. Your Common Sense, and your Crisis,[16] unquestionably awakened the public mind, and led the people loudly to call for a declaration of our national independence. I therefore esteemed you as a warm friend to the liberty and lasting welfare of the human race. But when I heard you had turned your mind to a defence of infidelity, I felt myself much astonished and more grieved, that you had attempted a measure so injurious to the feelings and so repugnant to the true interest of so great a part of the citizens of the United States. The people of New England, if you will allow me to use a Scripture phrase, are fast returning to their first love.[17] Will you excite among them the spirit of angry controversy at a time when they are hastening to amity and peace? I am told that some of our newspapers have announced your intention to publish an additional pamphlet upon the principles of your Age of Reason. Do you think that your pen, or the pen of any other man, can unchristianize the mass of our citizens, or have you hopes of converting a few of them to assist you in so bad a cause? We ought to think ourselves happy in the enjoyment of opinion, without the danger of persecution by civil or ecclesiastical law. Our friend, the President of the United States,[18] has been calumniated for his liberal sentiments by men who have attributed that liberality to a latent design to promote the cause of infidelity. This, and all

16. *The American Crisis* was a pamphlet series Paine wrote beginning in 1776, defending the cause of American independence. The famous first line of the first pamphlet said, "These are the times that try men's souls."

17. Revelation 2:4. Adams is referring to the revivals of the Second Great Awakening, which had recently begun.

18. Thomas Jefferson.

other slanders, have been made without the least shadow of proof. Neither religion nor liberty can long subsist in the tumult of altercation, and amidst the noise and violence of faction. *Felix qui cautus*.[19] Adieu.

7. ROGER SHERMAN, 1789

Of all the prominent Founding Fathers, Roger Sherman of Connecticut might have been the strongest evangelical Christian. He was a steadfast supporter of his pastor, Jonathan Edwards, Jr., the son of the great preacher and Calvinist theologian of the Great Awakening of the eighteenth century. Sherman was a signer of the Declaration of Independence and the Constitution. At the Constitutional Convention he also brokered the famous "Connecticut Compromise" regarding representation in Congress. But Sherman was also a very active layman in his church. In 1789, he published a meditation on communion, or the Lord's Supper, which is excerpted here. As skeptical as Jefferson, Adams, Franklin, and Paine may have been about traditional Christian doctrine, certain Founders like Sherman still not only believed in biblical theology, but they also actively promoted it.

From Roger Sherman, *A Short Sermon on the Duty of Self Examination* (New Haven, CT, 1789), 3–4.

. . . Do we rightly understand the mediatorial character, and the offices Jesus Christ is invested with, that he was appointed by the Father to undertake the work of redeeming lost sinners; and for this purpose was constituted a prophet to reveal the counsels

19. Latin phrase meaning "happy is he who is cautious."

of his grace;—a priest, by the sacrifice of himself to atone for our sin, and plead for pardon; and a king, to rule or reign over, and defend us; Have we right apprehensions of the covenant of redemption and grace; that the Father from all eternity, upon the foresight of the fall, determined to rescue and save a chosen number; and to this end, appointed his own Son to be mediator of the new covenant; to take upon him our nature, to be made under the law, and as the sinner's substitute, to obey the precepts, and endure the penalty thereof; thus fulfilling all the righteousness of it, for the justifying of the ungodly . . .

God most graciously offers, thro' Christ, to be again reconciled to us; to pardon our iniquities; to grant us the adoption of Sons, with all their present privileges and future blessedness; or, in the more comprehensive language of Scripture, that he will be to us a God, a God in covenant, to bless and make us happy forever.

But then on the other hand, in order to the enjoyment of these privileges, we are required heartily to consent to, and accept of this covenant, by sincerely repenting of all our Sins, believing in the Lord Jesus Christ, and by devoting ourselves unreservedly to his Service.

8. WILLIAM LIVINGSTON, 1786

William Livingston, the long-serving governor of New Jersey (1776–1790) and signer of the Constitution, was also an ardent Presbyterian. Like Samuel Adams and Patrick Henry, Livingston worried about the influence of Deist writers in America. Even before the American publication of Paine's *Age of Reason*, Livingston wrote the anti-Deist editorial excerpted here, which appeared in a number of

American newspapers in the late 1780s. He wrote under the pen name "Hortensius."

From the *New Jersey Gazette*, June 12, 1786.

For the New-Jersey Gazette

DEISM

Did you ever see a man, courteous reader, arrogating to himself the title of philosopher and of a profound thinker, who could not even give a definition of philosophy, nor ever had a serious thought in his life? . . .

Have you ever seen a man who ridiculed all faith and all mystery, and expected to obtain eternal felicity by practising the morality dictated by the light of nature, acknowledging at the same time his belief of the greatest absurdities in the world; and practicing no more morality than a horse? A man pretending to the acutest penetration and judgment; and yet not knowing how to doubt where he ought; to rest assured where he ought; and to submit where he ought?

Did you ever see a man who insisted that the bare light of nature was sufficient (and revelation consequently unnecessary) to conduct us at present in the path of duty, and to everlasting happiness hereafter; and in the same breath confessing, that, notwithstanding this light, (luminous and brilliant as he made it) a very great part of the world that has no other guide, is this moment involved in pagan superstition, and the grossest idolatry?

Did you ever see a man who denied the miracles wrought by Jesus Christ, though proved by a cloud of witnesses who sealed their testimony with their blood; and yet affecting to believe the fabulous wonders of Apollonius of Tyana, upon the credit of Philostratus, who has written a silly romance about that astrologer, which was never believed by any, save by those who believe every thing but what is true?[20]

Did you ever see a man who resolved all the moral attributes of the Deity into that of Mercy; and this mercy into a connivance at sin, and the virtual abolition of all his laws?

Did you ever see a man who flattered himself that the precepts, the morality and the history of our holy religion; the wonderful and unparalleled life and death of its author; the wisdom and sanctity of its injunctions; the authority and sublimity of the sacred writings; the testimony of ocular witnesses; the blood of so many martyrs; the accomplishment of so many prophecies; the attestation of so many miracles; the tradition of so many ages; the conversion of so great a part of the world to a religion renouncing the world, and propagated not only without, but against, external force; the perpetuity of the faith through a perpetuity of the most bloody persecutions; the impregnable foundation of the church; and all the other proofs in support of christianity, are answered and confuted, or rather totally annihilated by the unphilosophical philosophy of a Bollinbroke, or the wretched pun or thread-bare jest of a Voltaire, or a Rousseau? . . .

Did you ever see a man who denied the possibility of miracles, and yet demand[ed] a constant series and uninterrupted succession of them, to prove a divine mission?

Have you ever seen a man who reproached religion with all the horrors of persecution, and the fanaticism of the most sanguinary zealots, and at the same time acknowledging that these excesses were the evident abuses of christianity; and directly

20. Apollonius of Tyana was a first-century CE Greek philosopher who was reputed by his biographer Philostratus and others to have possessed miraculous powers such as the gift of healing.

repugnant to the peaceable spirit of the gospel, and the notorious inhibitions of its illustrious founder?

Did you ever see a man unable by the light of reason to reconcile the blemishes in the natural, and the disorders in the moral, world, with the idea of an all-wise and all-good governor of the universe—some regions for instance, almost deprived of the heat of the sun; others scorched by its insupportable splendor; winds, tempest and earthquakes, vulcanoes and inundations threatening universal destruction; the ocean overflowing the greatest part of the globe; and an immense quantity of its terra firma covered with rocks and mountains and desarts of land, incapable of cultivation; nor apparently formed for the sustenance of man or beast—and this same man able, by revelation, to reconcile all this; and yet scorning by revelation to do it? . . .

Have you ever seen a man, who, unable to prove, by the light of reason, the immortality of the soul; or that, from the intimate union between the operations of the soul and those of the body, the latter ceasing, the former will not terminate;—and able, by revelation, which hath brought immortality to light, to prove his eternal duration; and yet scorning by revelation to prove it?

Did you ever see a man who, unable by the light of reason to account for his own hopes of immortal happiness, from the absolute impossibility of reconciling, by the help of that light, the immutable justice of the Supreme Legislator, with the impunity of the transgressors of his laws (for as to the idea of the attribute of mercy, it is indubitably borrowed from revelation; and in the hands of those miserable reasoners, most miserably perverted) and who by revelation, could account for it; and yet scorning thus to solve this, otherwise inscrutable, enigma?

Have you ever seen such a man, sir? Why then you have seen a—blockhead.

9. ELIAS BOUDINOT, 1815

Elias Boudinot was a key patriot leader from New Jersey, a member of the Continental Congress and the U.S. House of Representatives, and the director of the U.S. Mint from 1795 to 1805. Boudinot, a devout Presbyterian, became increasingly alarmed about the rise of Deism and the attacks on traditional Christianity by Thomas Paine and others. He helped found the American Bible Society in 1816, and wrote Christian treatises such as *The Age of Revelation* (1801) and *The Second Advent*, which used prophecies from the Bible to argue that America risked losing the blessings of God if it continued to pursue infidelity.

Elias Boudinot, *The Second Advent, or, Coming of the Messiah in Glory* (Trenton, NJ, 1815), 530–533.

"And in the days of these kings, that is, of some of these kings, (the kingdoms of Babylon, Persia, Greece, and Rome) shall the God of Heaven set up a kingdom, which shall never be destroyed; and the kingdom thereof shall not be left to other people, but it shall break in pieces and consume *all these kingdoms,* and it shall stand for ever."[21]

Although the kingdoms and nations of Europe are first to be involved in this visitation from on high, yet even the United States of America have also reason to fear and tremble, when God shall arise "to shake terribly the earth." It is true, that their

21. Daniel 2:44.

constitutions have been long since formed and established on a purer basis.—The first settlers of this wilderness were the sons and daughters of banishment, flight, and persecution. This desart proved an asylum for the Church of Christ, when the enemy came in as a flood; then she flew into the wilderness, as on the wings of an eagle.

It is said to be a known fact, and if true, is a remarkable one, that the Congress of the United States, for near two years, were puzzling themselves to find a proper device for their great seal, which was also to serve as their arms, and their standard. Various committees were, from time to time, appointed, who brought in different reports, which were rejected, almost as soon as brought in; and it seemed that nothing on the subject could be proposed that was likely to give any tolerable satisfaction, till a motion was made and almost unanimously agreed to, that the Secretary should be authorized to determine on such device as he thought proper, which, without further confirmation, should become the arms and seal of the United States.—This was a very unusual measure for this body, who generally reserved every report for their own ratification, before it could take effect. The Secretary accordingly established the present seal and arms of the United States, to the great satisfaction of Congress, consisting of the American bald eagle, with expanded wings, and thirteen bars on his breast; in one claw a bundle of thirteen arrows, in the other an olive branch, and his head in a cloud surrounded by thirteen stars, with the motto, "*E pluribus unum*," out of many to form one. This appears to be very appropriate, as ready to receive the distressed of all nations, foster them under his wings—protect them by his power, and form one nation of them all.

But has not America greatly departed from her original principles, and left her first love? Has she not also many amongst her chief citizens, of every party, who have forsaken the God of their fathers, and to whom the spirit may justly be supposed to say, "ye hold doctrines which I hate, repent, or else I will come unto you quickly, and will fight against you with the sword of my mouth."[22]

America has been greatly favoured by God, in all her concerns, both civil and religious, and she has much to hope, and much to fear, according as she shall attentively improve her relative situation among the nations of the earth, for the glory of God, and the protection of his people—She has been raised up in the course of divine Providence, at a very important crisis, and for no very inconsiderable purposes. She stands on a pinnacle— She cannot act a trifling or undecided part—She must determine whom she will serve, God or mammon—She stands by faith, and has great reason to take heed lest she should fall, from a vain confidence in her own internal strength, forgetting "the rock from whence she has been hewed, and the hole of the pit, from whence she has been digged."[23]

Is she not divided into violent parties, full of deadly hatred to each other, contrary to the charitable spirit of the Gospel?—And will not God avenge himself for these things?

And if these should be the latter times of the fourth or Roman government, and the seven Churches of Asia mentioned in the Revelations, be any ways figurative of the seven periods of the 1260 years of the prophesying of the witnesses in sackcloth, or of the seven vials and the seven trumpets, as some good men have supposed, may not the address to the sixth Church, or that of Philadelphia, being answerable to the

22. Revelation 2:15–16.
23. Isaiah 51:1.

present period of the world, be applicable to the United States. "And unto the angel of the Church (in Philadelphia) write; these things saith He, who is holy;—He who is true;—He who has the key of David;—He who openeth, and no man shutteth; and shutteth, and no man openeth; I know thy works; behold I have set before thee an open door, and no man can shut it: for thou hast a little strength, and has kept my word; and hast not denied my name. Behold, I will make them of the synagogue of Satan, who say they are Jews, and are not, but do lie; behold, I will make them to come and to worship before thy feet, and to know that I have loved thee—because thou hast kept the word of my patience, I also will keep thee from the hour of temptation, which shall come upon all the world, to try them who dwell upon the earth. Behold, I come quickly; hold that fast which thou hast, that no man take thy crown. Him who overcometh, will I make a pillar in the temple of my God, and he shall go nor more out; and I will write upon him the name of my God, and the name of the city of my God, which is, *new Jerusalem*, which cometh down out of Heaven from my God; and I will write upon him my new name. He who hath an ear, let him hear what the Spirit saith unto the Churches."[24]

Hearken then, ye who are happily delivered from many of the evils and temptations to which the European nations are exposed. Your fathers fled from persecution: a glorious country was opened to them by the liberal hand of a kind Providence;— a land, literally, flowing with milk and honey;—they were miraculously delivered from the savages of the desert;—they were fed and nourished in a way they scarcely knew how. Alas! what have been the returns, their descendants, of late years, have made for

24. Revelation 3:7–13.

the exuberant goodness of God to them? The eastern states, however greatly fallen from their former Christian professions, were settled by a people really fearing God. "Remember therefore from whence thou art fallen, and repent, and do thy first works, or else I will come unto thee quickly and will remove thy candlestick out of its place, except thou repent,"[25] that is, will deprive thee of those Gospel privileges with which thou hast been so greatly favoured.

25. Revelation 2:5.

SELECTED BIBLIOGRAPHY

Adair, Douglass, and Marvin Harvey. "Was Alexander Hamilton a Christian Statesman?" *William and Mary Quarterly*, 3d ser., 7 (1955): 308–329.

Albanese, Catherine L. *Sons of the Fathers: The Civil Religion of the American Revolution.* Philadelphia: Temple University Press, 1976.

Allen, Brooke. *Moral Minority: Our Skeptical Founding Fathers.* Chicago: Ivan R. Dee, 2006.

Bell, James B. *A War of Religion: Dissenters, Anglicans, and the American Revolution.* New York: Palgrave Macmillan, 2008.

Beneke, Chris. *Beyond Toleration: The Religious Origins of American Pluralism.* New York: Oxford University Press, 2006.

Berens, John F. *Providence and Patriotism in Early America, 1640–1815.* Charlottesville: University Press of Virginia, 1978.

Bernstein, R. B. *The Founding Fathers Reconsidered.* New York: Oxford University Press, 2009.

Boller, Paul F., Jr. *George Washington and Religion.* Dallas, TX: Southern Methodist University Press, 1963.

Bonomi, Patricia U. *Under the Cope of Heaven: Religion, Society, and Politics in Colonial America.* Updated ed. New York: Oxford University Press, 2003.

Bonomi, Patricia U., and Peter Eisenstadt. "Church Adherence in the Eighteenth-Century British American Colonies." *William and Mary Quarterly*, 3d ser., 39 (1982): 245–286.

Borden, Morton. *Jews, Turks, and Infidels.* Chapel Hill: University of North Carolina Press, 1984.

Botein, Stephen. "Religious Dimensions of the Early American State." In *Beyond Confederation: Origins of the Constitution and American National Identity*, ed.

Richard Beeman, Stephen Botein, and Edward C. Carter, II, 315–330. Chapel Hill: University of North Carolina Press, 1987.

Buckley, Thomas E. *Church and State in Revolutionary Virginia, 1776–1787*. Charlottesville: University Press of Virginia, 1977.

Butler, Jon. *Awash in a Sea of Faith: Christianizing the American People*. Cambridge, MA: Harvard University Press, 1990.

Church, Forrest. *So Help Me God: The Founding Fathers and the First Great Battle over Church and State*. New York: Harcourt, 2007.

Commager, Henry Steele. *The Empire of Reason: How Europe Imagined and America Realized the Enlightenment*. Garden City, NY: Anchor Press/Doubleday, 1977.

Conkin, Paul K. "The Religious Pilgrimage of Thomas Jefferson." In *Jeffersonian Legacies*, ed. Peter S. Onuf, 19–49. Charlottesville: University Press of Virginia, 1993.

Cousins, Norman. *"In God We Trust": The Religious Beliefs and Ideas of the American Founding Fathers*. New York: Harper and Brothers, 1958.

Curry, Thomas J. *Farewell to Christendom: The Future of Church and State in America*. New York: Oxford University Press, 2001.

Curry, Thomas J. *The First Freedoms: Church and State in America to the Passage of the First Amendment*. New York: Oxford University Press, 1986.

Davis, Derek H. *Religion and the Continental Congress, 1774–1789: Contributions to Original Intent*. New York: Oxford University Press, 2000.

Dreisbach, Daniel L. *Thomas Jefferson and the Wall of Separation between Church and State*. New York: New York University Press, 2002.

Dreisbach, Daniel L., Mark D. Hall, and Jeffry H. Morrison, eds. *The Forgotten Founders on Religion and Public Life*. Notre Dame, IN: University of Notre Dame Press, 2009.

Dreisbach, Daniel L., Mark D. Hall, and Jeffry H. Morrison, eds. *The Founders on God and Government*. Lanham, MD: Rowan and Littlefield, 2004.

Evans, Bette Novit. *Interpreting the Free Exercise of Religion: The Constitution and American Pluralism*. Chapel Hill: University of North Carolina Press, 1997.

Feldman, Noah. *Divided by God: America's Church-State Problem—and What We Should Do about It*. New York: Farrar, Straus and Giroux, 2005.

Ferling, John. *Adams vs. Jefferson: The Tumultuous Election of 1800*. New York: Oxford University Press, 2004.

"Forum." *William and Mary Quarterly*, 3d ser., 56 (October 1999): 775–824. Includes: James H. Hutson, "Thomas Jefferson's Letter to the Danbury Baptists: A Controversy Rejoined," 775–790; Robert M. O'Neil, "The 'Wall of Separation' and Thomas Jefferson's Views on Religious Liberty," 791–794; Thomas E. Buckley, "Reflections on a Wall," 795–800; Edwin S. Gaustad, "Thomas Jefferson, Danbury Baptists, and 'Eternal Hostility,'" 801–804; Daniel L. Dreisbach, "Thomas Jefferson and the Danbury Baptists Revisited," 805–816; Isaac Kramnick and R. Laurence Moore, "The Baptists, the Bureau, and the Case of the Missing Lines," 817–822; James H. Hutson, "James H. Hutson Responds," 823–824.

Gaustad, Edwin S. *Neither King nor Prelate: Religion and the New Nation, 1776–1826.* Grand Rapids, MI: Eerdmans, 1993.

Gaustad, Edwin S. *Proclaim Liberty throughout All the Land: A History of Church and State in America.* New York: Oxford University Press, 2003.

Gaustad, Edwin S. *Sworn on the Altar of God: A Religious Biography of Thomas Jefferson.* Grand Rapids, MI: Eerdmans, 1996.

Guyatt, Nicholas. *Providence and the Invention of the United States, 1607–1876.* New York: Cambridge University Press, 2007.

Hamburger, Philip. *Separation of Church and State.* Cambridge, MA: Harvard University Press, 2002.

Hatch, Nathan O. *The Democratization of American Christianity.* New Haven, CT: Yale University Press, 1989.

Hatch, Nathan O. *The Sacred Cause of Liberty: Republican Thought and the Millennium in Revolutionary New England.* New Haven, CT: Yale University Press, 1977.

Heimert, Alan. *Religion and the American Mind.* Cambridge, MA: Harvard University Press, 1966.

Henriques, Peter R. "A Few Simple Beliefs: George Washington and Religion." In *Realistic Visionary: A Portrait of George Washington,* ed. Peter R. Henriques, 167–185. Charlottesville: University Press of Virginia, 2006.

Hoffman, Ronald, and Peter Albert, eds. *Religion in a Revolutionary Age.* Charlottesville: University Press of Virginia, 1994.

Holmes, David L. *The Faiths of the Founding Fathers.* New York: Oxford University Press, 2006.

Horwitz, Robert H., ed. *The Moral Foundations of the American Republic,* 3d ed. Charlottesville: University Press of Virginia, 1986.

Humphrey, Edward Frank. *Nationalism and Religion in America, 1774–1789.* Boston: Chipman, 1924.

Hutchison, William R. *Religious Pluralism in America: The Contentious History of a Founding Ideal.* New Haven, CT: Yale University Press, 2003.

Hutson, James H. *Church and State in America: The First Two Centuries.* New York: Cambridge University Press, 2008.

Hutson, James H. *Forgotten Features of the Founding: The Recovery of Religious Themes in the Early American Republic.* Lanham, MD: Lexington, 2003.

Hutson, James H. *Religion and the Founding of the American Republic.* Washington, DC: Library of Congress; Hanover, NH: University Press of New England, 1998.

Hutson, James H., ed. *The Founders on Religion: A Book of Quotations.* Princeton, NJ: Princeton University Press, 2005.

Hutson, James H., ed. *Religion and the New Republic: Faith in the Founding of America.* Lanham, MD: Rowan & Littlefield, 2000.

Jacoby, Susan. *Freethinkers: A History of American Secularism.* New York: Metropolitan, 2004.

Kidd, Thomas S. *God of Liberty: A Religious History of the American Revolution.* New York: Basic, 2010.

Kramnick, Isaac. "The 'Great National Discussion': The Discourse of Politics in 1787." *William and Mary Quarterly,* 3d ser., 45 (1988): 3–32.

Kramnick, Isaac, and R. Laurence Moore. *The Godless Constitution: A Moral Defense of the Secular State.* Expanded and updated. New York: Norton, 2005.

Lambert, Frank. *The Founding Fathers and the Place of Religion in America.* Princeton, NJ: Princeton University Press, 2003.

Levy, Leonard W. *The Establishment Clause: Religion and the First Amendment.* New York: Macmillan, 1986.

Levy, Leonard W. *Origins of the Bill of Rights.* New Haven, CT: Yale University Press, 1999.

Mapp, Alf J., Jr. *The Faiths of Our Fathers: What America's Founders Really Believed.* Lanham, MD: Rowan & Littlefield, 2003.

May, Henry F. *The Enlightenment in America.* New York: Oxford University Press, 1976.

McDonnell, Michael W. "The Origins and Historical Understanding of Free Exercise of Religion." *Harvard Law Review* 103 (1990): 1409–1517.

McGarvie, Mark Douglas. *One Nation under Law: America's Early National Struggles to Separate Church and State.* DeKalb: Northern Illinois University Press, 2004.

McLoughlin, William G. *Isaac Backus and the American Pietistic Tradition.* Boston: Little, Brown, 1967.

Meacham, Jon. *American Gospel: God, the Founding Fathers, and the Making of a Nation.* New York: Random House, 2006.

Mead, Sidney. *The Lively Experiment: The Shaping of Christianity in America.* New York: Harper & Row, 1963.

Miller, William Lee. *The First Liberty: America's Foundation in Religious Freedom.* Expanded and updated. Washington, DC: Georgetown University Press, 2003.

Morais, Herbert M. *Deism in Eighteenth Century America.* New York: Columbia University Press, 1934.

Munoz, Vincent Phillip. *God and the Founders: Madison, Washington, and Jefferson.* New York: Cambridge University Press, 2009.

Murrin, John M. "Fundamental Values, the Founding Fathers, and the Constitution." In *To Form a More Perfect Union: The Critical Ideas of the Constitution,* ed. Herman Belz, Ronald Hoffman, and Peter J. Albert, 1–37. Charlottesville: University Press of Virginia, 1992.

Noll, Mark A. *Christians in the American Revolution.* Grand Rapids, MI: Christian University Press, 1977.

Noll, Mark A., and Luke Harlow, eds. *Religion and American Politics: From the Colonial Period to the Present.* 2d ed. New York: Oxford University Press, 2007.

Noll, Mark A., Nathan O. Hatch, and George M. Marsden. *The Search for Christian America.* Westchester, IL: Crossway, 1983.

Noonan, John T., Jr. *The Lustre of Our Country: The American Experience of Religious Freedom*. Berkeley: University of California Press, 1988.

Novak, Michael, and Jana Novak. *Washington's God: Religion, Liberty, and the Father of Our Country*. New York: Basic, 2006.

Pencack, William. *Jews and Gentiles in Early America, 1654–1800*. Ann Arbor: University of Michigan Press, 2005.

Peterson, Merrill D., ed. *The Virginia Statute for Religious Freedom: Its Evolution and Consequences in American History*. New York: Cambridge University Press, 1988.

Powell, H. Jefferson. *The Moral Tradition of American Constitutionalism: A Theological Interpretation*. Durham, NC: Duke University Press, 1993.

Powell, H. Jefferson. "The Original Understanding of Original Intent." *Harvard Law Review* 98 (1985): 885–948.

Ragosta, John. *Wellspring of Liberty: How Virginia's Religious Dissenters Helped Win the American Revolution and Secured Religious Liberty*. New York: Oxford University Press, 2010.

Sanford, Charles B. *The Religious Life of Thomas Jefferson*. Charlottesville: University Press of Virginia, 1984.

Sheridan, Eugene R. *Jefferson and Religion*. Charlottesville: Thomas Jefferson Memorial Foundation, 1998.

Slauter, Eric. *The State as a Work of Art: The Cultural Origins of the Constitution*. Chicago: University of Chicago Press, 2009.

Staloff, Darren. *Hamilton, Adams, Jefferson: The Politics of Enlightenment and the American Founding*. New York: Farrar, Straus and Giroux, 2005.

Stark, Rodney, and Roger Finke. "American Religion in 1776: A Statistical Portrait." *Sociological Analysis* 49, no. 1 (1988): 39–51.

Stone, Geoffrey R. "The World of the Framers: A Christian Nation?" *UCLA Law Review* 56 (2008): 1–26.

Stout, Harry S. "Religion, Communications, and the Ideological Origins of the American Revolution." *William and Mary Quarterly*, 3d ser., 34 (October 1977): 519–541.

Thompson, Mary V. *"In the Hands of a Good Providence": Religion in the Life of George Washington*. Charlottesville: University Press of Virginia, 2008.

Waldman, Steven. *Founding Faith: Providence, Politics, and the Birth of Religious Freedom in America*. New York: Random House, 2008.

Weinberger, Jerry. *Benjamin Franklin Unmasked: On the Unity of His Moral, Religious, and Political Thought*. Lawrence: University Press of Kansas, 2005.

West, John G., Jr. *The Politics of Revelation and Reason: Religion and Civic Life in the New Nation*. Lawrence: University Press of Kansas, 1996.

Wills, Garry. *Under God: Religion and American Politics*. New York: Simon & Shuster, 1990.

Wilson, John F. *Public Religion in American Culture*. Philadelphia: Temple University Press, 1979.

Wood, Gordon S. "Religion in the American Revolution." In *New Directions in American Religious History*, ed. Harry S. Stout and D. G. Hart, 173–205. New York: Oxford University Press, 1997.

Wood, James E., Jr., ed. *The First Freedom: Religion and the Bill of Rights*. Waco, TX, J. M. Dawson Institute of Church-State Studies, 1990.

Wuthnow, Robert. *The Struggle for America's Soul: Evangelicals, Liberals, and Secularism*. Grand Rapids, MI: Eerdmans, 1989.

INDEX